Ditching Your Debts

by G.B. Clark

Loompanics Unlimited
Port Townsend, Washington

8-24-95

This book is sold for information purposes only. Neither the author nor the publisher will be held accountable for the use or misuse of the information contained in this book.

Ditching Your Debts
© 1995 by G.B. Clark

Cover by Dan Wend

Published by:
Loompanics Unlimited
PO Box 1197
Port Townsend, WA 98368
Loompanics Unlimited is a division of Loompanics Enterprises, Inc.

ISBN 1-55950-112-X
Library of Congress Card Catalog 94-73082

Contents

ACKNOWLEDGMENTS

For their continued support and encouragement to complete this book, special thanks to:

My wife, Sue Ann, our daughter Bonnie Kay, our son Clinton.

Special thanks to David E. Lloyd, Doug Allen and Don Siemon for their encouragement, sharing and caring.

Also, thank you to Kathleen Johnston for her help.

For publishing this book, thanks to everyone at Loompanics Unlimited, who helped make it possible.

Quotations used in the book come from: *The Home Book Of Quotations Classical and Modern*, Eighth Edition, By Burton Stevenson, Dodd, Mead & Company, New York.

Historical information about scot-free comes from: *Morn's Dictionary of Word and Phrase Origins*.

Writing a book sometimes involves much research. This research cannot be done without the availability of a library and the reference staff. So, I say THANK YOU!, to the reference staffs at the following libraries:

Everett Public Library, Everett, Washington
Harrison Memorial Library, Carmel, California
Monterey Public Library, Monterey, California
Pacific Grove Library, Pacific Grove, California
Rohnert Park Public Library, Rohnert Park, California
Santa Rosa Central Public Library, Santa Rosa, California
Sno-Isle Regional Library System,
    Lake Stevens, and Marysville Branches, Washington
Sonoma State University Library, Rohnert Park, California

Without libraries and the able assistance of the library reference staffs, most non-fiction writers would be up the creek without a paddle.

DEDICATION

I dedicate this book to all people who have any debt problems. Sometimes, the only solution left is to ditch your debts, much like tossing excess cargo overboard. About half of this book provides information on how to avoid credit problems. The other half deals with possible solutions to existing credit problems.

The reader will learn about choices.

- Avoiding credit problems.
- Options if you have credit problems.
- Negotiating problems with your creditors.
- Ditching your debts, legally.
- Walking away from it all.

Good luck in whatever course of action you decide to follow. However, please remember this important information:

DISCLAIMER

The author and publisher are not lawyers and do not advocate the breaking of any laws. Certain activities listed in this book might violate local, state, or federal laws. *This book reports such information to demonstrate examples of what people have done.*

This information is not a recommendation that you follow the same actions. You need to get information and protect yourself. You should check with an attorney or legal authorities before taking any particular course of action. You will want to make sure that you do not violate any laws.

Preface

This book will provide you with information, so you can decide from two or more alternatives. Good decisions usually arise from two or more alternatives. I want you to have the tools to examine your particular circumstances and be able to decide what will benefit you.

Why would anyone want to ditch their debts in the first place? The reasons might be many. Maybe a person becomes tired of marriage, family, job, creditors, unemployment, or a particular lifestyle. All of those are possible contributing factors to "D-SAD." That is a term I coined for Debt-related Stress, Anxiety, and Depression.

This book is not an indictment of the credit system. However, most of the problems facing people today have to do with money. Money, either as credit or hard earned cash, is the root of many problems facing people today. Therefore, money becomes a suspect. In that sense, the whole credit system must come under scrutiny. The credit system in the United States has become an out of control monster. The credit monster eats people. This is a monster with no concern or regard for consumer well being. It is a monster interested in numbers, feeding off the people.

The credit system regularly entices or encourages people to charge beyond sensible family budget guidelines. Credit card companies constantly barrage cardholders with special offers to purchase various items. There is a constant effort to encourage people to spend money they do not have. Television, radio and print media tell us to buy now, pay later.

Buying now and paying later can become a sickness that is spreading everywhere, like a contagious disease. Sadly, many people get sucked in by this constant encouragement to spend. The monthly payments do not rise that much as you add new purchases to your total debt.

It is possible for your debt to grow, almost unseen. Some people spend here, spend there, and they do not pay too much attention to it. The debt is there, but not readily recognizable until they no longer have the wage earning capacity to pay their debts. The inability to cope with debt is a leading factor in suicide.

The average two income family that suddenly loses the income of one wage earner is in serious trouble within about two months. The reason for this is the lack of adequate cash reserves. The experts recommend that we should have savings of six to eight months' gross income. This savings account will be our contingency fund. Very few people can afford to do this, because so many people live from paycheck to paycheck. To illustrate this, from about 1981 to 1992, the savings percentage dropped from about 8% of our earnings to about 2% of our earnings. American workers are saving less. That means we are either spending more, or having to pay more to exist.

There are people who have very good incomes, very good job stability, and very clean credit. However, these people are the exception, not the rule. If a family earns $5,000 to $10,000 per month, they should have very few problems getting along in life. However, there are many people who have this income and higher, and can't manage their finances properly because they have too much debt.

Many couples, young and old, are taken in by the credit system, only to find the monthly payments are soon out of reach. Many loan companies feed off the hardship that individuals and families endure. How many people do you know that are frequent users of companies that specialize in personal loans? More than one person is too many. It is likely to be someone out of a job that needs a small loan to tide them over until their situation improves.

Such loans usually require some type of security. It could mean getting a loan, secured by nearly all of their personal property. Personal loans carry a very high interest rate, and sometimes there are loan "costs" or "origination fees" that add to the total amount borrowed. Most personal loan lenders push credit life insurance on the borrower.

This type of life insurance coverage usually has a very high cost in relation to the amount of coverage. Lenders call this type of insurance a "profit center." That means the lender will earn a very high commission from the insurance you buy. This insurance is a "hidden expense." That means the lender will be very happy to add the insurance premium to the loan amount. That way, the borrowers do not actually see the dollars go out of their pocket. Usually, this type of insurance is not worth the extra cost.

The bankruptcy courts have millions of files that will fairly document what I speak of in this preface. So, if you are interested in *Ditching Your Debts*, you will not be alone. There are millions of people out there with circumstances very similar to yours.

Introduction

—————◆—————

When economic times change from good to bad, many events can happen. From 1986 through 1994, many companies laid off millions of employees. You hear it on the evening news or read about it in the paper. Companies cut from 100 to 2,000 jobs (people) from the production force.

Not all job loss happens with hourly or salaried workers. One big company cut 20,000 management jobs over a certain period. Many people have their wages cut back, or their hours cut back, and sometimes both. These actions have the net effect of fewer dollars in the pay envelope. Sometimes people lose their jobs. With reduced pay, or no pay at all, it is very easy to fall behind in your regularly scheduled monthly payments.

Nearly all people spend beyond their earning capacity — that is nothing new. Plastic money, *a credit card*, makes it easier to spend beyond your earning capacity. It's not very easy to spend cash you do not have, unless you bounce checks, and that is against the law!

Unfortunately, the recent history of most credit card companies is to encourage people to go further into debt. The credit card companies accomplish this by granting the card user increased limits. Also, various companies extend more credit by offering pre-approved, new cards.

Your prompt payment of your monthly bill, over time, allows a credit card company to believe you should have more credit. More credit comes by other card companies issuing you a pre-approved card, or by your present cards increasing your credit limit. However, what happens when a person's income changes or stops? What happens when people cannot keep up with their payments? You can read an actual case history in the next chapter.

Credit card companies still encourage people to spend money they do not have. Within the present credit card system, there are no alternatives to not being able to pay your debts. If you do not have a job, regardless of the reason, and can't pay your bills, credit card and collection companies will come after you. As long as you continue to make your monthly payments, everything will be okay.

However, if you fall behind one month, they will be on the phone to you very fast. The past several years, most credit card companies have "fine-tuned" their collection departments. Now, there are levels of customer contact, ranging from very friendly, "we want to help you" approaches to the rough "pay, or else we will have to...." approach. It is very sad to realize one potential problem associated with debt. Sometimes when people get further into debt, it is easier for them get access to more credit cards.

In late 1994, Department of Labor statistics reveal there are about *nine to ten million* people out of work. Actually, the number of unemployed is much higher. There are many people who cannot qualify for unemployment insurance. In addition, there are many thousands of people who give up looking for work. Also, many thousands of people are no longer counted, because their unemployment benefits expire!

(Somehow, the Department of Labor conveniently omits these unemployed from the statistics. Many people now live in the "cash society" or are homeless, and are not a part of the statistics. Many of these people scratch out a bare existence by working for barter, casual wages, or "cash-under-the-table." These people are not part of the statistics as underemployed or unemployed, because the system no longer recognizes them.)

Some people believe there are about 25 million "unemployed" people in this country. As an example, let's say that about nine million unemployed have an average of about six credit cards each. These cards have credit limits at an average of about $1,000 per card. That could mean there is an "unemployed debt" figure of 54 BILLION dollars.

EMPLOYMENT DISPLACEMENT "JOBS LOST"

TIME, September 9, 1991 Business, Pg 54, 55.
The Economy "Permanent Pink Slips"

"...experts say nearly half the 1.6 million jobs the economy has lost in just the last 13 months may never be restored."

"Number of net layoffs 6/90 through 7/91 — 2,111,000 "

FORTUNE, February 24, 1992 THE ECONOMY, Pg 52.

"...An estimated 1.6 million jobs have been lost to date...680,000 of those were the result of downsizing...the pace will quicken through 1992 and will continue long after the economy begins to recover." Comments attributed to Dan Lacey, Editor, *Workplace Trends*.

TIME, July 20, 1992 Business, Pg 64, 65.
"The Great American Layoffs"

"...So far this year, corporate America has shed an average of 1,500 positions a day." Comment by Mitchell Fromstein, President, Manpower, Inc.

"...fewer than 25% of U.S. companies have completed the task of downsizing...the U.S. could face up to five more years of job losses at the searing rate of 375,000 a year."
Comment by Joseph Hanotta, Chairman, Jannota, Bray.

BUSINESS WEEK, July 26, 1993, Economic Trends, Pg. 20.
"DOWNSIZERS CHALK UP A RECORD FIRST HALF"

"...Corporate America unveiled plans to do away with close to 255,000 jobs, 23% more than in the same period last year, and the largest first-half tally ever. Comments by James E. Challenger, President, Challenger, Gray & Christmas, Inc.

Figure 1

If about nine million unemployed people have trouble paying their bills, they might owe from $12,000 to $18,000 each, not counting a home mortgage. Therefore, if an average unemployed household's consumer debt is about $15,000, there is a range of about 54 to 135 billion dollars of "possible distressed debt" in the United States.

These millions of people with debt trouble are trying to survive the best way they can. They are potential candidates for bankruptcy. These people are vulnerable, and they are having their lives turned in a negative direction. One of the main causes of this is easy credit. Another cause is the continual encouragement by the credit card companies for these people to spend more and more and get further into debt. Most everyone has seen or heard the various commercials used by the credit card companies. These ads mention how easy it is to spend "money," practically anywhere in the world! Unfortunately, too many people want to spend money they do not have. They believe the commercials and buy their dreams now. However, paying for the dreams later can be a problem.

Nearly all credit card companies earn money in two ways: they charge the merchant a service charge against all credit sales. Sometimes there is an "enrollment fee" which I am not counting, although this fee does generate income for the credit card companies. The second source of income is from interest and late payment charges paid by the card holder. Most credit card companies are money making machines. They do not have feelings, nor do they care about your personal financial problems.

The credit card companies need to develop an alternative plan for people out of work. Otherwise, these companies could experience very large losses. This will be due to the financial failure of so many card holders. Such losses might be a gigantic lesson in humility for many of the money hungry credit card companies.

Nowadays, the typical business philosophy of most credit card companies has a narrow focus. Most of these companies are rigid and unimaginative about solutions to this emerging national problem. Most card companies, and their assigned collectors, constantly harass credit card holders in arrears. Most credit card companies are out for one thing and one thing only: *your money*, plain and simple. These companies are greedy and do not care about the people that become a casualty of uncaring policies. The constant pandering of most of the credit card companies leaves many people with terrible financial problems. Something must be done to protect the unemployed from losing everything they have due to problems with the credit system.

Family financial difficulties sometimes lead to stress, depression and despondency. Credit problems can cause family unrest, divorce, child and spousal abuse, even suicide. Statistics show big increases in suicide attempts and successes during bad economic times. It is sad to see that people can be driven to the brink of personal disaster because of the debts they owe. Further, it is despicable for the hounding by bill collectors and credit card companies to result in personal tragedy.

I am writing this book with the hope of providing you with alternatives. These alternatives will show you other ways of dealing with financial hardship, including *Ditching Your Debts*, if that becomes necessary.

Often, people with money (PWM) look down their noses at people with financial troubles. PWM are often quick to place blame. "The people with credit problems should have, could've, if such and such would've happened." Very few PWM take the time and interest to help others, but there is at least one notable exception: Percy Ross. Mr. Ross is a millionaire. He gives money to many of the people who write and ask for help. Of course, he cannot honor every request. After all, he is just one person, among the many People With Money.

You may write to
PERCY ROSS
P. O. Box 39000
Minneapolis, Minn. 55439
Include a phone number if you wish. All letters are read. Only a few are answered in his column, although others may be acknowledged privately.

Figure 2

There is some barnyard philosophy to explain Mr. Ross' generosity. That is: "Money is like manure. If you let it pile up and sit there, it will stink. On the other hand, if you spread it around, a little here, a little there, it will help make everything grow."

Most people view financial difficulties or hardship differently. I know of a person whose attorney advised him to file Chapter 7 bankruptcy (complete discharge). The man had only $3,500 in debts! What drove the guy nuts was the constant phone calls, at home and at work, to pay up *or else!* He only had six credit cards, and had been off work for three months.

However, once he got behind, he could not catch up with his payments. The constant harassment by the credit card and bill collection companies almost drove the man crazy. His relief was to file BK (bankruptcy), though it would be on his credit record for about 10 years.

Another person I know of had *$76,000 in credit card debts!* She had good equity in her home, and could refinance through alternative lenders. They charge a higher rate for a shorter term than normal, or conventional financing. She kept trying to reduce the debt on her 42 credit cards, but could not do that. The interest meter, running about 18% to 22%, made the debt grow much larger each month. She sold her home and ended up with a small amount of cash. However, there was not enough money to help reduce her debt. The last I heard, she was interviewing bankruptcy attorneys.

While bankruptcy is a last resort for many people, it remains the least favorite choice for the average person. There is a stigma about bankruptcy in this country. Many people think they should drain their finances and virtually be homeless before seeking BK protection.

Still others will suffer much hardship and never file BK, continuing to suffer with or endure the hardship. Yet there are many "wealthy people" who filed BK in the past. You don't see them pushing a grocery store cart, looking for cans and bottles and sleeping in an alley. BK is one of the alternatives you will learn about in this book. However, you also will learn other methods to deal with credit problem situations.

1
Setting The Stage:
A True Story

"Truth will ultimately prevail where
there is pains taken to bring it to light."
— George Washington

"Bob Smith," age 37. Married, with three children. Bob and his wife were buying their home. Bob earned $18,000 per year. His wife did not work, because of the young ones at home. Bob and his wife had several credit cards and a few accounts with local merchants. The limits of their cards ranged from $750 to $1,500. They paid their bills on time and had an excellent credit rating.

Then Bob lost his job. Although this was not his fault, Bob was not eligible for the weekly unemployment benefits that most people would receive. As a result, Bob and his wife had to resort to their meager savings as an income source. This paid their living expenses while Bob looked for a new job. Their savings allowed them to pay all their monthly expenses on time.

However, their savings began to dwindle rapidly. It became necessary to juggle their monthly payments, including the house payment. Within three months, most of the monthly payments, including the mortgage payment, were 60 days late. At this point, Bob and his wife sought and received a second mortgage on their home.

A mortgage broker arranged this private money loan for the Smiths. The loan was for 13% interest for only five years. The loan cost 10 points, plus title and escrow fees, etc. This totaled about $4,800 in loan fees. This loan served as a cash resource to bring all payments current and leave some residual money for living expenses.

Bob continued to look for work, but did not have any luck finding a job. Maybe he was too old, too experienced, too well-educated, or maybe he did not have enough experience, etc. Bob heard all the excuses possible. This was during a bad economic time. Bob and his wife prepared a budget. They saw they had four months of food, utilities, phone, insurance and auto expenses, plus two months of first and second mortgage payments. At this point, they decided to try to sell their home, in a very depressed real estate market.

It took five months to sell their home, and just a few moments away from foreclosure. The home, valued at $125,000 for the second mortgage appraisal, sold for $95,000. With all the transaction fees and loan prepayment penalties, the Smiths had a few thousand dollars left. They used most of that money for moving and storage, and first, last and security deposit for a rental home. By this time, all their creditors started dunning by mail and phone. Bob is an honest person and tried very hard to explain his situation.

None of the creditors were kind-hearted. They all wanted, *demanded*, their money immediately, or else. Not just the payments that were behind, but the *whole amount*. Bob offered to work off the debts, but the retail stores responded that such an offer was not a criteria for their hiring of employees. At this point, Bob felt a growing hostility toward himself for letting the situation develop. He also felt hostility toward the credit card companies for being so rigid. Bob felt frustrated about the situation, because he wanted to do something to resolve the matter. Yet he was unable to do anything about it.

Soon process servers appeared with summonses to small claims court. The retail stores, credit card and bill collection companies were very persistent. The credit card and bill collection companies added their costs to the amounts owed by the Smiths. These costs included: court fees, process service fees, and attorney fees. These amounts owed, with interest and penalties, grew at a big rate each month.

The Smiths had two cars, an older car they owned, and a newer car they leased on a four year contract with a bank. The bank repossessed the newer car when the Smiths missed two car payments. A big surprise came when the bank sent the Smiths a bill. *The bank wanted the full amount of the contract, plus costs!* Several creditors continued to call every day. Some of the collection agencies called several times a day.

The feelings the Smiths had were bad enough, even without the continued insults from the bill collectors. Being without a job and almost dead broke does not bring much happiness. The mood was made worse by the constant demands for payment, even at night and on the weekends. The Smiths finally had their phone number changed to a new, unlisted number, which effectively stopped the dunning by phone. However, mail dunning increased via certified and registered mail. Also, some of the collection companies put in personal appearances at the Smith residence, the collectors demanding all or part of the debt owed. They went away empty handed. One collector said he was willing to accept five dollars toward the amount owed! Bob told the collector they had five dollars, but it had to go for food. Bob explained that he had to put the family first, ahead of the collector's client. That made the collector clear out very fast.

When the escrow closed on the sale of their home, the Smiths put most of their belongings into storage. They used a local branch of a nation-wide moving company. This was very expensive — $1,800 to move the items to the storage facility, plus $1,200 for three months secured storage. However, these fees included the moving company taking the items out of storage and delivering the items to an address in the local area. The cost of storing the items nearly wiped out all the money that remained from the sale of their home.

The Smiths decided to store their remaining belongings because they planned to stay with relatives who lived nearby. The Smiths could stay there until they found a house to rent. However, the relatives' house was very small with no garage or storage space, and that house was up for sale. The Smiths were able to stay there only two months, until the escrow closed on that home.

Creditors were not quick enough to get a judgment and have it filed with the county recorder during the title and escrow work on the sale of the Smiths' home. Normally, a title company examiner will find such a recorded judgment. Had that been done, the Smiths would not have had any money at all!

During that two month period, the Smiths were free of bill collector activity. When they moved from their previous home, they left no forwarding address to the relatives' home. During that two month stay, Bob rented a Post Office box in a nearby community. Following postal regulations, Bob had to give his present address, and that was the address of the relatives.

When the Smiths moved again, it was to a community about five miles from their relatives. The Smiths signed up for water, gas and electricity, and an unlisted phone number. They had to pay for the first and last months' rent, plus security deposit. Now the Smiths had less than $200 left. They moved into the two bedroom home and unpacked. As they were getting accustomed to their new surroundings, something interesting happened.

Within two days of moving in, there was a process server at their door. With a grin from ear to ear, the process server said how hard it was to find the Smiths. You could tell he took great pride in locating them, at last. The process server carried summonses from two of the retail stores. Within one week, more summonses arrived. The collection hassle nightmare started again. Somehow, signing up for utilities had tipped off the collection agencies.

Bob appeared at the court hearings and tried to explain his situation, again making an offer to work off the debts. The retail stores did have outlets in the area. It would have been simple for Bob to work off the debts. Bob considered the offer to work off the debts as an honorable solution to the situation. However, the retail stores again stated that working off credit owed was not a criteria for employment. The municipal court judge had much sympathy for Bob's predicament. However, the judge, by law, had to side with the creditors.

Soon, nearly all the Smiths' creditors took action to get judgments against them. This did not stop the in-person collection attempts or constant demands for payment. More summonses arrived by personal service, requiring Bob to appear at a "creditor's hearing." At that hearing Bob would have to answer all sorts of questions about himself. Bob appeared at the hearing and was given a lengthy form to complete — 18 pages in all!

The questions were about his life history from birth to present. Questions included: where he lived, attended school, worked, banked, etc. There were many questions about property, money, jewelry, guns, hobbies, and nearly anything that might have any value associated with it. Bob refused to answer most of the questions. He filled in his name, present address, and the fact that both he and his wife did not have jobs at the time. The rest of it was nobody's business.

Bob also stated, under oath, they had no savings or investments of any kind. Also, he said they had no cash value on life insurance policies. He also stated that a checking account in a local bank had less than a $50 balance. All the information was correct. (It is important to tell the truth in court.)

The person who requested the hearing, the local collection agency representative, was furious. In fact, the man became so enraged, he yelled and stomped out of the hearing room. He went back to the judge's chambers to complain to the judge about the "uncooperative examinee!"

A few minutes later, the collection agency person returned with the attorney who represented the collection agency. The lawyer asked for the information and was given the same report from Bob. Bob also said the rest of the questions had nothing to do with the $950 owed to the retail store. Bob said he would be very willing to discuss the whole matter with the judge and let the judge decide if the questions were pertinent or not. At that point, the lawyer backed down and told the collection agency man to forget about it.

This caused the collection agency man to become enraged again. This time, his face became purple and veins popped out on his forehead. He threatened to get even with Bob, no matter how long it took. At this point, the attorney had to remove the man from the room.

Circumstances finally forced the Smiths to apply for welfare (AFDC), through the county's social services. This provided the Smiths with food stamps and a small cash grant to help pay the rent. Bob still looked for work every day, but didn't find anything. He finally resorted to doing volunteer work for a few organizations within the county, and at a church. He did this as a way of paying back what he received in the way of welfare aid.

Bob was also aware that such volunteer work could provide a lead to a job. Therefore, Bob worked as hard as he could, no matter how demeaning or insignificant the work appeared to him.

The Smiths could not keep up with their rent payments and had to move again. This move put them into a larger, older home that was somewhat rundown. College students had occupied the house. They left the place in a filthy mess. It took two days of hard work for the Smiths to get the house clean enough so they could move into it. The landlord saw how hard the Smiths worked to clean up the place and was very appreciative. In addition to a slightly lower rent, he did not ask for a security deposit or the last month's rent in advance.

The landlord was a little reluctant to put the utilities in his own name. However, he finally agreed to do that when the Smiths assured him they would pay the utilities with the monthly rent. Another bonus came when the landlord agreed to have the rent paid in two installments each month, to coincide with the welfare payments. *With this move, the Smiths did not use a forwarding address, and the utilities were not in the Smith name.*

Mrs. Smith found a part-time job, which reduced the AFDC grant by the amount she earned. Bob succeeded in finding a few temporary jobs. Some of the jobs were for just one day, while others were for as much as a week or two. They reported all of their income to the welfare department. Then the welfare department deducted the wages from their AFDC grant.

The Smiths had a very close friend order an unlisted phone in his name, for the home the Smiths rented. This is a very important factor in getting any kind of work — having a phone. It looks like most employers are not too willing to hire or trust someone who does not have a telephone!

Nothing associated with initiating utility service at the new residence was in the Smith name. For all intents and purposes, no one, except a few trusted relatives and friends, knew where the Smiths lived. On job applications, the Smiths always listed their P.O. Box as their address. They mentioned they would supply the street address upon request.

This was done in case a prospective employer decided to check with the local credit bureau. Some employers actually do that. Of course, there are ways to track the phone number to an address. However, the Smiths believed that a phone in another person's name would throw off someone from the credit bureau doing a casual check.

A bad credit report can prevent you from getting a job in some cases. That is not fair. On one hand you can have the good intention of getting a job so you can pay the bills. On the other hand, employers can deny you a job because of the bills you are trying to pay.

Through diligent searching of various records, the process servers, collection agencies and the credit bureau soon learned the Smiths had a P.O. Box. (Probably through an employer checking with the credit bureau.) Soon dunning letters and summonses started to arrive in the mail.

Bob took some pleasure in refusing first class mail that looked like a dunning letter. (Any first class mail sent to your home or P.O. Box can be refused... simply dash a line through your name and address and write or print *REFUSED* in large letters. Present regulations require the postal service to return refused mail to the sender.)

Some of the mail Bob received looked like checks. Other mail looked like court documents, except the return address did not show a name. Instead, the return address listed only a number and street. Some of the mail really looked suspicious. Many letters looked like an invitation or announcement. Bob refused all mail that required his signature. After three tries at delivery on certified/registered mail, the postal service must return the letters to the sender. The postal service stamps the mail UNDELIVERABLE.

The Smiths lived in that old house for a full year, and had "quiet enjoyment of household." Of course, along with the peace and quiet they also had the agony of being jobless and broke. When a person or family is jobless and without any money, Christmas is probably the most depressing experience of the year.

Someone reported their plight to the local Catholic Church. Although the Smiths were not Catholics, at Christmas they received an ample food basket. They were able to prepare a turkey dinner with the all the trimmings, from the items in the basket. That particular gift was a feast, allowing Christmas spirit to take on a new meaning!

Much the same way that sand has to leave the upper part of the hourglass, the Smiths finally had to act, on December 27th. They could not find work, other than part-time jobs and occasional temporary work. The Smiths realized their credit rating was beyond repair. There was no way they could catch up with or pay their bills.

Now, they only had one choice left: bankruptcy. On the advice of an attorney who counseled welfare recipients, the Smiths filed for relief under United States Bankruptcy laws.

(An interesting point to mention here is this: an attorney advised the Smiths to file bankruptcy *before selling their home*. However Bob was very strong-headed about trying to pay their debts in full. He ruled out filing for bankruptcy. If they had filed *before* selling their home, they would have had more assets protected, including equity in their home. They would have been ahead, emotionally and financially).

The Smiths completed all the forms and documents necessary for a bankruptcy. They did all the work themselves. They did not have the money to hire an attorney for a fee. The Smiths purchased a book about bankruptcy from a book store and got the forms from the county Legal Aid Society. The directions were very clear, and the whole project was almost a simple task.

It was not financially possible for the Smiths to hire legal help. They could not see why they should pay from $85 to $500 or more to have an attorney represent them, because they had so few assets remaining. However, the Smiths did seek the advice of an attorney who specializes in bankruptcy law. The attorney charged the Smiths only $25 to review their paperwork and make sure everything was correct.

The following June, the BK court granted Mr. and Mrs. Smith relief from all their debts. Their debts totaled less than $18,000. No one can lay specific blame, other than that the Smiths had allowed themselves to fall into the credit trap. While the Smiths had good income, they charged more than they should have. They also went for higher limits offered by the credit card companies. The real irony was, the more the Smiths owed, the easier they could get credit as well as higher limits on their existing cards!

Another very serious error on their part was using cash advances from credit cards for living expenses.

Bankruptcy for the Smiths was a real first-class embarrassment. There was a lot of agony and the need for a lot of soul searching before they decided what to do. Some of the items involved in their decision included:

1. Even if Bob found a job earning close to what he did before he lost his old job, *it would take many years to repay their debts.* This was due to the way interest and late penalties accumulate and add to the remaining balance.

2. Not one retail company or bank credit card offered a workable solution to the problem. Not one bank or credit card company would accept Bob's offer to work off the debt.

3. If Bob had succeeded in finding a job, there was a better than 50-50 chance he could lose it. Many firms will fire someone due to excessive wage attachments. At many companies, an employee with more than two wage attachments will lose their job.

4. Certain types of employers might not have considered Bob for employment. This was because of the debts he owed and the bad credit record on file. This information is accessible to nearly every credit bureau throughout the country. (Credit bureaus share information regionally, and nationally. They are like a big vacuum, sucking up all the dirt they can find.)

5. The Smiths knew that bad credit would remain on their credit report for up to several years. The BK discharge would stay on their credit report for up to 10 years. They knew their credit rating was terrible, so it did not matter if they filed for BK. That made it a little easier for them to decide to file BK. After the BK, they could work to reestablish some types of credit, and always pay on time.

The credit system heartily encouraged the Smiths to run up their debts. There were the special promotions included with the monthly statements, in addition to increased credit limits. Needs beyond their control forced the Smiths to overextend their credit. Yet the credit system became vicious, squashing efforts by the Smiths to regain some self-respect by working out a solution to their debt problems.

The Smith example is not an isolated case, especially now that consumer debt has reached an all-time high. There are millions of people faced with nearly the same circumstances. The past several years reflect a downturn in the economy. When the economy declines, it usually means poor or very marginal employment opportunities.

The recent layoffs in many industries could be just a small breeze before the storm. As an example, the rippling effect of unemployment in the auto and housing industries can be very massive. How many jobs are there in the auto, housing and peripheral industries? Think about that for a moment. You can see how many people might lose jobs very quickly, when the economy "slows down."

After their BK, the Smiths did slightly better. Bob found a job at a hotel, at minimum wage. However, the job included one meal and some snacking on breaks. This helped their food bill at home. Bob was glad to get that job, despite his several years of business management experience and his college degree in business administration. Mrs. Smith found a better job in a child care center. Through both jobs, the Smiths barely met their modest monthly debts. They both worked very hard to earn $150 more per month than they received on AFDC, while they looked for work. Is there a message here?

Five years later, the Smiths saved enough money for a modest down payment to purchase a home. They assumed a high balance FHA loan. The future looks very good for the Smiths. They might get credit cards in the future. If they do, the Smiths assure me they will be extremely careful how they use those cards!

2
The Quickest Way
To Ditch Your Debts

"Without a rich heart, wealth is an ugly beggar."
— Emerson

The quickest way to ditch your debts also has the most long-term side effects. Bankruptcy is the fastest way to spell relief if you suffer from credit problems. BK hangs around on your credit report for just about TEN YEARS! However, do not despair. If your financial situation changes a year or two after your BK discharge, lenders will review your situation based on merits. I know of people who successfully applied for home mortgages 26 months after BK discharge.

The lenders will want to know the reason for the BK. *You have to prove that it was a circumstance beyond your control.* That means the lenders will want to see a business failure, or some type of medical problem, as the chief cause of your BK. If you used credit cards and could not pay the bills, most lenders will not want to do business with you. It is not exactly easy to reestablish credit after BK. However, rebuilding credit will be discussed in another chapter.

You should be on guard with companies that tell you they can get rid of a BK on your credit report. These firms usually want a lot of money up front. Many people doubt those firms will be successful in getting rid of that type of derogatory information from *all the credit repositories* (credit reporting agencies). If not removed from all credit repositories, the information will surface again, and continue to do so. However, the older the BK discharge, the less lenders and credit card companies are concerned about it.

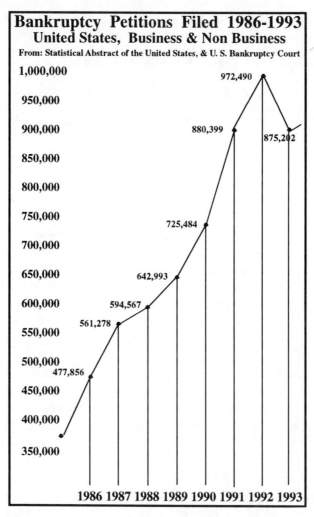

Figure 3

You should only consider BK as a last resort. There are other tactics to try before filing BK, and those will be discussed in another chapter. If you are at the point where you need to cut to the chase, then BK is the answer. Remember, BK is there to help you solve a problem. Do not feel guilty about seeking help. Shame comes from failing to ask for help when you should. Some of America's leading citizens have found it necessary to declare BK, so you are not alone.

The following is very good information which you should read quite carefully...

What Can I Do, If I Can't Pay My Debts?

The following information is published in the public interest by the State Bar of California, and is reproduced here by permission of the State Bar of California.

1. *What Can Bankruptcy Do For Me?*

Bankruptcy is a way to get out of debt when you owe more money than you can be expected to pay in the near future. We have come a long way since the time of the debtor's prison when your creditor could have you jailed until you paid a bill. Today, the law allows an honest debtor to have a court "discharge" or cancel most of his or her debts in order to make a fresh start. This form of bankruptcy is sometimes called a "straight" bankruptcy.

You can use bankruptcy to discharge your debts no matter how you got into debt, as long as you were honest. Maybe you used credit cards and built up a large number of bills. Perhaps you or your spouse lost a job and have not been able to pay your rent or make your car payments for several months.

Bankruptcy usually means that most, and sometimes all, of your debts will be canceled. And except for debts that you *must* pay (see #7), going through bankruptcy generally stops your creditors from "garnisheeing" or taking your wages. This means your employer cannot be forced to give part of your salary to your creditors to help pay off your discharged debts.

However, bankruptcy will not solve all of your money problems. If you are out of work, bankruptcy can cancel your old debts. But you still must find a way to pay new bills. And, although it is not likely, going through bankruptcy may mean that some of your possessions will be sold so the money can be given to your creditors. Also, remember that you are not allowed to have your debts discharged again for six years.

2. *What If I Just Need More Time To Pay My Debts?*

An alternative to bankruptcy, called the Chapter 13 plan, lets you pay off part or all of your debts over a period of time under court supervision. Usually, you can take up to three years to pay. But in some cases the court gives you as long as five years.

You can use a Chapter 13 plan if you have a steady income. This means you can be a wage earner, the owner of a small business, or someone who receives a pension, social security or welfare benefits.

Whether you are a wage earner or own a small business, you must owe less than $350,000 in "secured" debts and less than $100,000 in "unsecured" debts.

A secured debt means you have a written agreement that offers a creditor some of your property as security. If you own a car, it might be the security. If you do not pay the debt, the secured creditor can take your car. A house or furniture are other common forms of security. With an unsecured debt, no security agreement is made.

Once you file under Chapter 13, your creditors cannot sue you for the money you owe them. They also are not allowed to write or telephone you demanding payment. And the court will not sell your property in order to pay either your secured or unsecured creditors.

Remember: Under Chapter 13, you do *not* have to agree to pay your debts in full. If you are unable, or do not want to pay all the money you owe, the court may approve a plan under which you offer less — say 50 cents on the dollar — paid out over three years.

If your Chapter 13 payments should become too difficult to make, it is possible to have them lowered, get more time or take time off from making payments. What if you have a major problem before all of your debts are paid? You might have a long illness or lose your job.

Then you can switch from Chapter 13 to straight bankruptcy. When you file straight bankruptcy, the court may cancel some or all of your remaining debts.

3. *How Can I Set Up A Chapter 13 Repayment Plan?*

A lawyer can help you write a plan that tells how you intend to pay part or all of your debts. Later, he or she can help you show the court why the plan is a good one for you. The plan must be filed with a bankruptcy petition and the proper fee, in the bankruptcy court. You may file alone, or a husband and wife may file jointly. The fee is the same whether you file alone or together, and it can be paid in installments through your plan. Your lawyer's fees, which the court will set, also can be paid through your plan.

When the court approves your plan, it will assign a person called a "trustee" to handle your payments. The trustee and your lawyer will explain how your repayments will be made.

If the court allows you to repay only a part of your debts, "priority claims" must be paid in full unless those creditors say you can pay less. Priority claims include secured debts and any federal or state income taxes that you have owed for the past three years, as well as the court costs and trustee and attorney fees involved in setting up a Chapter 13 plan. If you own a business, there may be other priority claims to pay.

4. *Can I File Straight Bankruptcy At Anytime?*

Yes, as long as your debts were not discharged less than six years ago.

As soon as you file the proper bankruptcy forms in court, you can stop making payments on your old bills, except for alimony and child support. This is allowed even though your debts may not be canceled officially for several months.

Remember: This does *not* apply to most secured debts you may have.

The law says your creditors are not allowed to garnishee your wages, sue you or bother you with letters or telephone calls asking for payment. If your creditors do not believe you have filed for bankruptcy, ask them to call your lawyer or check with the bankruptcy court.

5. *How Do I Start A Bankruptcy Action?*

You or your lawyer will have to file bankruptcy forms with the nearest U.S. Bankruptcy Court.

You must give a lot of information on the bankruptcy forms. You must tell about your income, bank account, tax returns, real estate, personal property and much more. And if you make mistakes, some or all of your debts might not be canceled.

For example, you must make a list of all your "assets." These are cash, stocks, bonds, real estate (land or a house), cars and any other property you own. You also must list your debts and creditors. The creditors who are listed with their correct names and addresses are called "scheduled creditors." The money you owe them can be canceled by bankruptcy. However, creditors listed incorrectly or not listed at all are called "unscheduled creditors." Your debts to unscheduled creditors generally will *not* be canceled.

A lawyer can help you fill out the forms and then represent you in court. If you do not know a lawyer, you can ask your friends, a co-worker or an employer to recommend one. Business and professional people such as bankers, doctors, ministers and teachers may be able to give you a lawyer's name.

Or call your local Lawyer Referral Service or Lawyer Referral & Information Service. Look in the Yellow Pages of your telephone directory under "Attorney Referral Service," "Attorneys" or "Lawyers." The person who answers your call can make an appointment for you to see a lawyer. Usually, you will pay a small fee to talk with a lawyer for about half an hour. If you want the lawyer to do more work for you, the bankruptcy court will set the fee.

You can also check the Yellow Pages and newspaper advertisements for a lawyer who may be able to help you. Perhaps you belong to a "legal insurance" plan through your company, labor union, credit union — or as an individual. Your plan may cover the work you need.

For more information on locating a lawyer, see *How Can I Find And Hire The Right Lawyer?*, published by the State Bar of California.

Once bankruptcy forms are signed, they must be filed with the clerk of the U.S. Bankruptcy Court. You and your spouse may file jointly on the same forms. The court will tell you what the filing fee will be.

6. *How Long Does It Take To Go Through Bankruptcy?*

After your bankruptcy papers are filed, you can stop paying your creditors even though your debts will not be discharged for about four months. However, if any creditor objects to having a debt canceled, it may take longer.

About 30 days after your bankruptcy papers are filed a "meeting of creditors" is held. Creditors do not have to attend because they are represented by the trustee. But you must be there and testify under oath. Your lawyer will tell you what papers to bring with you. The trustee and any creditors who attend the meeting can ask questions about your assets and debts.

If the trustee decides you must give up some of your property in order to pay part of the money you owe, both you and your creditors can object before the trustee's decision becomes final.

If your creditors or the trustee can prove that you have done something wrong, your debts will not be canceled. These are some of the reasons your debts might not be discharged.

- You lied about your assets.
- You intentionally gave false information on the bankruptcy forms or to the trustee, such as purposefully failing to list a creditor.
- You failed to obey a court order.
- You transferred or hid an asset during the last year in order to keep your creditors from getting paid. Maybe you put your savings account in your daughter's name.

Once the judge has decided any disputes between you and your creditors, your debts will be discharged within 90 days.

7. *Will All My Debts Be "Discharged" Or Canceled?*

This depends on the kinds of debts you have. The law says that these debts cannot be discharged even if your creditors do not object to having them canceled:

- Debts to unlisted creditors—the ones you did not list correctly on your bankruptcy forms or who do not know about your bankruptcy—in most cases cannot be canceled.
- Most income taxes and related penalties for the last three years.
- Some student loans that become due within five years of filing. However, if the bankruptcy judge believes that repayment will be too difficult for you or your family the loan may be discharged.
- Child support and alimony payments.

There are other debts that will not be discharged in bankruptcy if your creditors object and the court says they should be paid. However, they might be discharged if you file a Chapter 13 plan instead of straight bankruptcy. These debts include money you owe because:

- You made a false written financial statement. Perhaps you told the bank that loaned the money that you had no debts when you actually did.
- You obtained money or property by fraud. If you paid for a refrigerator by check when you knew you had no money in your checking account, you may have committed fraud.
- You took property that belongs to someone else. Maybe you offered your television set as security to one of your creditors and then sold the set to raise cash.
- You intentionally hurt another person or damaged someone's property on purpose.

8. *If My Loan Payments Are Discharged, Will My Co-Signer Have To Pay?*

Yes. A co-signer is a person who made a legal agreement to pay off your debt if you fail to do so. And he or she is responsible for the debt even if you file bankruptcy. What if you have a Chapter 13 plan? Then your creditors cannot ask your co-signer to pay off a loan as long as your Chapter 13 plan is in effect and says you plan to pay the loan.

9. *What If I Want To Pay Certain Debts?*

Perhaps you are making payments on a loan. Maybe you have paid $4,500 and owe only $600 more. In this case, you may want to "reaffirm" or agree to pay the debt, even though it might be canceled during bankruptcy. Maybe one of your creditors asks you to continue paying off a certain debt. You can agree to "reaffirm" this debt, although you do not have to. Be sure to discuss reaffirmation with your lawyer.

If you decide to reaffirm a debt, the law says you can change your mind within 30 days. Also, reaffirmation is permitted only before your debts are discharged. When you want to reaffirm a debt, the court will hold a hearing to make sure you understand that you do not have to pay the money. And if the court believes repayment of a *consumer* debt will be too difficult for you, it will not let you reaffirm.

10. *What Happens To My Property When I Go Through Bankruptcy?*

Occasionally, you might have to give up some of your property. However, most of your possessions will be "exempt" under law. This means they cannot be sold to pay your creditors. Your lawyer will help you make a list of your exemptions. If the trustee or your creditors object to any items on your list, the court will hold a hearing. You will not have to give up any money you earn after you file your bankruptcy papers or anything you buy with that money. But, if you receive a refund for income taxes paid during any year before you filed bankruptcy, the money might be used to pay your creditors.

11. *Which Assets Will I Be Able To Keep?*

This depends on whether you choose federal or state exemptions. In California, you have a choice. And the amount of property that is exempt can double if both you and your spouse file bankruptcy. In fact, if you like, you may choose federal exemptions while your spouse takes state exemptions.

These are some, but not all of the federal exemptions:

- A $7,500 interest in a home and/or burial plot. What if you do not own a home or burial plot? Federal law says you can still use the $7,500 exemption. In fact, you can add $400 to it and claim

$7,900 worth of additional exemptions in any kind of property. Even if you do have a house and burial plot worth $7,500, you can claim $400 worth of extra exemptions in other property. You can use this exemption too, to keep a refund on income taxes that you paid before the year you file bankruptcy.

- A $1,200 interest in *one* car or other motor vehicle.
- Any items worth up to $200 *each* in these categories: Household goods and furnishings, clothing, appliances, books, animals, crops and musical instruments.
- $500 in jewelry.
- $750 worth of books or tools that you need for your work.
- A life insurance policy.
- Health items, such as a hearing aid, that were prescribed for you.
- Social Security and veteran's benefits.
- Unemployment insurance proceeds.
- Pension and profit sharing plans.

If you choose California exemptions instead, you will be able to keep, among other things:

- Up to $45,000 equity interest in a home.
- The household furnishings and clothing that your family needs.
- A car worth up to $500 more than any money you owe on it.
- Up to $2,500 in tools that you need for your work.
- $1,000 in a savings and loan account, but not in a bank account.
- $1,500 in a credit union savings account.
- A cemetery plot.

You should know that in some cases, these assets may not be exempt. Suppose you bought a car or a television set and signed an agreement promising the return of the property if you cannot keep up the payments. In this case, you will not be allowed to cancel the debt and keep the property. You can keep it *only* if you pay the entire balance owed or the present value of the property, whichever amount is less.

Important note: What if you are involved in a lawsuit? Make sure your lawyer knows that you intend to file bankruptcy, and tell your bankruptcy attorney about your case. Any court action you will be involved in can help your lawyers decide the best time to file your lawsuit and whether you will be better off choosing straight bankruptcy or Chapter 13.

The General Purpose Of This Pamphlet Is To Provide General Information To The Public. It Is Not Intended To Give Legal Advice Regarding Any Specific Problem. Readers Should Know That The Law Is Complex And Constantly Changing. Therefore, Anyone With A Specific Legal Problem Should Consult An Attorney.

If you would like an original copy of this pamphlet, write to:

State Bar Pamphlets (B)
Communication Division
555 Franklin Street
San Francisco, CA 94102

There is no charge for one copy of this pamphlet. However, as a courtesy to the State Bar of California, this author urges you to include a self-addressed, stamped, business-size envelope. Also, whether or not you live in the state of California, I urge you to include one dollar to help cover handling.

3
The Evaluation

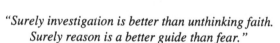

"Surely investigation is better than unthinking faith.
Surely reason is a better guide than fear. "
— R. G. Ingersoll

The point of this book is to provide enough information to enable you to evaluate your particular situation, then plan a course of action. You have to have decision-making tools before you decide what to do. If you owe money to many creditors, they might hound you all the time. You need to decide what you should do.

There should be no fear, guilt or shame in trying to do what the Smiths did. You can "get lost" for a short time, to give yourself some breathing space. It is okay to hide for awhile. This will give you time to think about your situation without people calling you or writing you or showing up in person, demanding that you pay. You should be proud knowing that you decided to sort matters out and eventually take a course of action. In effect, you have called "time-out" on your particular circumstance.

If you are fortunate enough to still have a job, or get a job right away, you might be able to get back on your feet quickly. This will allow you to avoid the legal measures necessary to protect yourself. Even if you do have employment, it might be necessary to get the legal information required to protect your wages and property. You might benefit from the financial counseling services that are available to you. You might get help with matters such as budgeting your household income. (Speaking of budgeting your household income, I know of a couple who earn a total of $5,875 per month. However, they have no savings and very little in their checking account. They do not have many debts. Their problem is spending. They spend all their money on clothes, hobbies and eating out!)

Whether you have a job or not, facing increased debts or problems associated with paying your present debt load can be very frustrating. If you cannot cope with the situation, you must begin a process of self-examination. You must place emphasis on what is important and necessary to meet your immediate needs and the needs you will have within the next few weeks and months. You should put yourself on trial. The outcome of the trial might allow you to suffer a long sentence, a short sentence, or get off "scot-free" to a certain extent.

(Here's a little trivia for you. The term scot-free dates back to Elizabethan times, when the local government official, usually the sheriff, collected a sceot pronounced "scot" from everyone. The sceot was a tax. So you could have something scoet-free. That meant you either did not have to pay any taxes on it, did not pay any taxes, or avoided paying any taxes on it. Today, scot-free translates to doing something without having to suffer any punishment or pay for it.)

Part of the evaluation concerns budgeting. Therefore, here are some tips on budgeting.

Budgeting

One of the main priorities during this evaluation period is to make an assessment of your finances. You must determine the value of your assets and items you have *paid for in full*. These are items you can quickly convert to cash. It is better to use very conservative figures when estimating the cash value of your items. If you paid $500 for a color television set when it was new two years ago, you might be lucky to sell it for $50 to $100.

The more cash you realize from such a sale, the better. However, when you figure your near cash assets, you should count the value of the television set as $50 or $100. It might make you feel somewhat dismal, selling something for a low price, when you know it is worth much more. However, that is the price one must pay sometimes, in order to put food on the table or pay the rent. Once you have a reasonable determination of your finances, you should prepare a simple budget.

The budget should be for one month at a time. It would not hurt to plan a few months ahead, so you might realize what to expect for the next three or four months. In preparing the budget, you should be as realistic as possible about your expenses.

Here are some items to include: rent, food, utilities, car expense, insurance (if you still have it), and non-food necessities. Also, you should budget a small amount for entertainment, and job search expenses, if applicable. Once you list your expenses, compare those against your income and cash on hand. This will tell you whether the overall money situation is positive or negative.

Be very careful when considering the habits you maintain. Smoking two packs a day, visiting a bar twice a week, smoking pot, etc., are expensive habits. The idea here is to stop smoking, etc., entirely, or short of that, cut way back. These "addictions or habits" are very costly. Eating out is very expensive, even when you buy sliced meats and cheeses from the local deli. You should learn to avoid "packaged" foods at the store, especially frozen dinners and similar "convenience" foods. The point here is *survival!*

If you are in a time of survival, you will need all the cash you can get. Cigarettes, beer, soda, eating out or buying convenience foods every day, all add up to many dollars each week. Even pumping your own gas saves a little bit on the gasoline expense. At this point, you have to consider S.O.S. That is, *Stop Over-Spending!*

People who are continually in debt might want to consider investing in a few visits to a psychologist. It might be worth it to attempt to determine what "triggers" the craving to buy. Once you identify those "triggers," you can deal with them. Many psychologists have a fee schedule based on one's ability to pay. Some areas might provide free counseling to the poor or unemployed. Remember, there is no shame in asking for help. You win half the battle by recognizing there might be a problem and being willing to get some help in finding the solution.

All of us have heard about compulsive drinkers, compulsive gamblers, compulsive eaters, etc. Have you heard about compulsive spenders? You could be a compulsive spender if you:

1. Have trouble paying your rent or house payment.
2. Spend more than 25% of your monthly income on charge cards or contract payments.
3. Have trouble resisting certain sale items because they are a good buy or "the price is right."
4. Buy items you do not really need.
5. Use charge card advances or bank advances to make up for cash shortages, or to help with living expenses.
6. Have trouble maintaining or building a savings account. *You should think about it, before you buy anything.*

Impulse buying is a major objective of the process of *merchandising.* It looks like many men overspend because it fits part of a "macho" image. This could take the form of spending money around their male friends. Other times, the spending might involve impressing women. Some spending might be done to impress one's family. Women might overspend in an attempt to make themselves look prettier. Advertising conditions many women to think or believe they should look and appear like magazine cover models.

Such desires can lead to substantial overspending, especially in department stores. The main problem comes from going crazy with credit cards. Credit card shoppers at department store sales or special events often spend money without giving any thought to the matter. Such careless spending on credit cards might eventually take away money needed within the home.

You need to realize what your expenses are. Then you need to learn how to cut back and save money. Once you can look at your assets, you can determine your staying power. If all you have is the money to cover one week's expenses, you are in serious trouble. It is not easy to find solutions to these problems within one week. The longer your cash staying power, the better your chances of success.

More cash will allow you to get out of your present predicament, whether it is personal or financial.

Job Search

If you are not working, another part of the evaluation is taking inventory of your job skills. During the evaluation period, it is of prime importance to locate a job. With so many people out of work and actively looking for work, the competition can be very tough. You need to determine your strengths and weaknesses by taking a personal inventory of your job skills and work experiences.

Prepare a list of your job skills and work experiences. Next, prepare a list of your strong points and be ready to emphasize these when you apply for a job. Although the main purpose of the evaluation period is to determine your financial strength, do not lose sight of the goal. The goal is a new or better job, either in your present location or in a new location.

Job Search Tips

When looking for work, you have to get organized. Know ahead of time what types of jobs you should be seeking. Determine where those jobs might be. Also, develop a list of secondary job considerations. A secondary job is one in which your job skills, work experience and education do not matter, as in jobs like driving a cab, dish washing, etc.

You have heard the saying "First impressions are usually correct," or "First impressions count." This is very true in searching for a job. This means having clean clothes without wrinkles, clean shoes, neat hair, and an overall good looking, business-like appearance. Men should have a good shave, or a neatly trimmed beard. An auto repair shop or construction site might not care about your appearance. However, a firm with a sales or management position will probably expect you to look presentable.

Again, remember that many employers *do not check employment references.* On the other hand, many jobs, by their nature, will require a reference check.

Experience

You should tailor your résumé to the job you want or seek. The application may contain questions about previous experiences. Base your answers on your experiences. Show how your background will help in the position for which you are applying. (NOTE: If you decide to get lost, you might not be able to disclose your most recent job. A reference check to your immediate past employer might lead someone to your new location!)

A job you held two years ago might be okay to use as a job reference, because that employer probably wouldn't know about your recent job activity. If you have to develop a fake job history, and are keeping your real name, you could use *some* of your real job history. (More on fake job history in another chapter.)

Of course, if you decide to change your name, your past employers become unusable as references. If you do develop a fake job history, you will not be the first person to do so. This is not something I recommend. I mention the subject because people do it, in their attempts to get a job.

Another item to look out for is your immediate past employer. That employer might be getting a lot of nuisance calls about you from bill collectors and credit bureaus. Your last employer, or fellow workers, might be happy to give collectors details about your past or new activities.

There is one sure way to get around the immediate past employer as a job reference. It is easy to say that you worked for your father or uncle. Then you say he died, and the business closed at your mother's or aunt's request. If necessary, you could provide the name and address of the foreman who would verify your position, pay and job performance. Of course, the "foreman" will be the name of a trusted friend who can help you in this situation. Also, you could have a secretarial service respond to a mail inquiry. (More on that in another chapter.)

The most important point about the job search is actually *getting out and looking for a job*! Regardless of how depressed you might feel about your situation, you need to start a routine. You must get up every morning, get out, and start looking for a job. *DO NOT* apply by phone. *DO NOT* send a résumé. *YOU MUST APPLY IN PERSON.* If you knock on enough doors, one will open for you. Do not take no for an answer. Keep checking back, in person, to see if there are any openings.

After five or six visits from you, the average employer will get the idea that you are very serious about working there. Very often, they will try to find something for you. Trust me, it works!

Success or Not?

In continuing the evaluation, let's say you are successful in finding a job. After you pay your monthly expenses, you have $200 left to spend as you wish. You can use this $200 in a few ways. First, you can spend part of this money on contingencies, such as unexpected expenses. What are those? Car repairs or medicines are examples of unexpected expenses. If the entire $200 is at your disposal, you could pay off part of your bills.

As an example, suppose you have $6,000 in debts. You now want to start paying $200 per month on those debts. It will take you about three and one-half years to pay off the $6,000. (This includes a 1.5% monthly charge on the unpaid balance). Over a period of 40 months, you will have a charge of about $1,870 in interest, not counting any late fees. Late fees could easily add another $700 to the total debt.

At this point, you must focus on two concerns. First, the thing that will improve your situation most is an increase in wages. This will allow you to pay larger amounts and reduce your balance more quickly. Second, if you are a probationary employee, you may not advance to permanent status. If you lose your job, you will be right back where you started.

The monthly payment of $200 does not allow for any savings, contingencies, or future unemployment. Most people, rightfully, will consider it an obligation to pay the $6,000. However, they may be placing themselves into a type of "slavery" by continuing to pay the debt as service fees and late charges add to the balance.

If your debts are higher than $6,000, you can see it will take a long time to pay off just those debts. What kind of an existence would that be? You must give some thought as to how long you are going to have to pay on your debts. Think about the service charges and late fees, and ask yourself if it is feasible to continue. Are you willing to continue?

In *Credit And Collections* (David McKay, Company, Inc., NY), author John W. Sede writes: "There is one major hazard in lawsuits and indeed in all vigorous collection efforts. Since most of your collection problems are people who are unable to pay — because of bad luck, lost jobs, poor financial management, getting in over their heads, major illness — the debtor who is long overdue with you probably owes money to lots of other creditors, too. He hopes against hope that he will be able to work things out eventually. But if you or other creditors press him too hard, he may declare voluntary bankruptcy."

This book, published in 1977, has a focus toward business owners. The book provides information on how business owners should go about credit and collections. The significance of the above quote is: *If you push too hard as a creditor, you might lose everything for yourself and the rest of the creditors.* It is a warning to creditors about not getting too aggressive in their collection efforts. Others would disagree, saying you should be the most aggressive of all the creditors, otherwise you might not get anything. That belief is that constant collection efforts will usually result in some kind of payment, if not payment in full. Most creditors would prefer to have something rather than nothing.

A recent example of this is a person I know who owes a little more than $5,000 on a credit card issued by a large bank. He got hurt on the job, was unable to work for a long time, and got into a real financial mess. He owed several months' back payments on all of his credit cards. He finally found a job. Somehow, the bank found out about his new job. They called him at work about twice a week. They offered to accept payments of $250 per month. He said it just wasn't possible, since he also owed ten other credit card debts. After several negotiations, this big bank settled on payments of only $25 per month. "Something is better than nothing." The last time I talked with this man, he had seen a BK attorney, and was contemplating filing BK.

If you try to pay off $6,000 at $200 per month, some creditors might agree with your proposed payment plan. They might agree to stop collection efforts, stop dunning, etc. In most cases they will not voluntarily suspend the monthly finance and service charges, on the grounds they have the expense of "carrying" your account. That is a bunch of horse manure!

When looking at the chance of losing everything versus having the principal fully repaid, most creditors should be willing to agree to your repayment plan. But don't count on all creditors being co-operative. It might do some good to threaten BK. On the other hand, it might not do any good at all.

In the Smith example, whenever they mentioned BK, creditors *IMMEDIATELY INCREASED* their collection efforts and summonses to appear in court. Therefore, before starting some type of voluntary repayment, you will need to consider three areas. Those are: Financial counseling, Chapter 13 BK or Chapter 7 BK. Let's take a look at each of these alternatives and determine how they could benefit you.

Financial Counseling

There are many financial counseling service firms. Most of these firms charge a fee for their work. The fees vary, but can amount to ten percent of your monthly income or more. However, some of these firms do not charge, or charge a sliding scale for their counseling. Private individuals own some of these firms. Also, banks, credit bureaus and collection agencies might own some of them.

Normally, someone at the counseling firm will review your income and living expenses. This is done to determine what money is available to pay your creditors. The counseling firm will attempt to get all your creditors to agree to equal, smaller, monthly payments. The counselor may or may not be successful in getting the interest and late fees waived on your behalf. Also, you will have the credit counseling fees added to your monthly payments.

There is a danger in dealing with such firms. Normally, you hand over your paycheck to such an organization. They pay all of your bills. *You run the risk of becoming a second class consideration.* The first class consideration is, of course, all your creditors. There have been vast numbers of people victimized by such credit firms.

When your debts are very high, the monthly interest and service charges continue to rise at an alarming rate. Very often, your monthly payment will not be enough to cover the interest and late charges. You could be in a situation where you will never be able to pay the debt completely. No matter how much you pay on your debts, or to the financial counseling service, your debts can continue to grow.

In some instances, it looks as though the firms providing counseling services do so for their profit. It looks like their sole purpose is to extract every possible dollar from the people owing the debts. Some credit counselors may be unethical. They ask the debtor to reduce living expenses to the absolute minimum while providing as much of the person's income as possible to the creditors. The credit counselor should represent *your* best interests. Instead, under the pretense of helping you, the credit counselors are really helping your creditors.

If the counseling service insists on controlling your finances, this could lead to trouble. There may not be much empathy or understanding about contingency expenses. You may not be able to purchase something you really need, because the counseling service controls your money. Often, the result in such matters is BK. The person might have been better off by filing BK much earlier.

Sometimes, counseling services are not successful in getting the interest and late charges stopped. It is not always in their interest to do so. Of course, there are exceptions. There are financial counseling services that work diligently to do a good job under adverse circumstances.

Not all the financial counseling services will have their hands out for your money. Some of these counseling services provide free counseling because of private financing by the credit industry. Some of these firms can be very helpful in giving you ideas on how to budget your earnings and where you should go for legal assistance. The outside opinion of someone who deals with financial problems might be just what you need. However, nearly everyone who is having financial trouble realizes the mess they are in and know they should turn to someone for help or advice. The fact remains that if the shoe fits, you should wear it. That means you can probably deal with the situation yourself. Knowing what the Smiths went through should clue you in on what you might have to do by yourself.

Again, not all financial counseling services are bad. Although many people get ripped off by such services, there are probably a great many people who have benefited from them. It looks like a few bad apples can ruin it for the rest. Most agencies will help prepare a budget for you. Other agencies might be extremely helpful in stopping wage attachments or creditor harassments.

In some instances, the agency may help you renegotiate your debts so your monthly payments will be more manageable. The counseling agency may be able to get the interest and late charges stopped. Sometimes there is a fee for this service. Other times, the service may be free. Remember, the main responsibility of such a service is to keep you from going into BK. Also, these services want to make sure you pay as much as possible toward eliminating your debts.

In order to get further information about financial counseling and consumer credit counseling, you can contact the following:

National Foundation for Consumer Credit, Inc.

611 2nd Avenue

Silver Spring, MD 20910

Phone: (301) 589-5600

Also, this organization is affiliated with the Consumer Credit Counseling Service national referral line, 1-800-388-CCCS (2227).

That phone number has a computer linked to incoming area codes. When you call that number, a computer will inform you about the CCCS office located nearest to you. Next, the computer will tell you the address and phone number of that office. Other options will allow you to check for other offices nearby, or for offices in other area codes.

You can use their advice and help to whatever extent possible in your situation. Please remember to include a stamped, self-addressed, business size envelope when you write for information from any group or organization.

An alternative to a financial counseling service or agency is to have an attorney set up a debt collection plan for you. If you have sufficient income to pay your debts within one or two years, such a plan may be acceptable to your creditors. The attorney could function much the same way as the financial counseling services. The attorney would receive your paycheck and make payments to your creditors, and to you for your living expenses.

For this type of service, the attorney will charge a fee. The attorney will probably set the fee as a percentage of your total debts. Usually the attorney will bill you monthly, just like the rest of your creditors.

It could be much more time saving for the attorney to set up the plan and leave the payment procedures to you. The attorney might be able to negotiate favorable conditions such as reduced amounts owed, or no interest or late charges. Then it would be up to you to stick to the program. Make sure that you have the income necessary to undertake such a plan. Remember, be sure you have the self-discipline to make the plan work.

The next chapter, *Legal Considerations,* will cover bankruptcy.

4

Legal Considerations

> *"'Tis a sluggard's part not to know what he may lawfully do."*
> — Seneca

The Attorney

Attorney or lawyer selection can be simple. Under the heading of "Attorneys" in the *Yellow Pages*, you will usually find many listings for lawyers that serve your area. Among the advertisements, you will notice specialized areas of practice by various attorneys. There will be headings such as "personal injury," "wrongful death," "worker's compensation," "bankruptcy," and others.

(By the way, do you know why they bury lawyers 22 feet, 5 inches underground? Well, most lawyers, *deep down*, really are very good people!)

Contact some offices of attorneys who specialize in bankruptcy. You will get general information about the nature of the services they provide. You will learn whether or not they can help you with a debt consolidation. Usually, attorneys do not charge for this initial information. Most attorneys might provide a fifteen to thirty minute consultation at no charge. Some may charge $25 to $50.

After several conversations, you will learn about the going rate for fees. Also, you will get an opinion about a particular attorney you think can help you the most. Unfortunately, there are no hard and fast rules for selecting a *good* attorney.

Word of mouth is a good form of advertising, whether it be a good or bad recommendation. If friends or relatives used an attorney with good results, that might be a good recommendation. However, that person might not have experience in the intricacies of BK. It may be better to work with a specialist. (A podiatrist has a M.D. Nevertheless, you probably would not want that person to remove your appendix.)

An attorney with a specialty in preparing wills and estate probation might be a terrific person and have an excellent record in that field. However, that attorney might have limited knowledge of BK laws. Therefore, the person who specializes in BK could advise you better about matters such as debt consolidation.

If your plan made by a financial counselor or attorney fails, you still have the option of BK. If you decide to file BK, remember that BK does not mean you automatically lose everything you own. Indeed, many items are exempted during the BK proceedings. Many people do not understand the full range of protection offered under the BK laws. BK laws may exempt many belongings people fear losing. Remember, the laws are constantly changing. That is why it is so important to check with a BK attorney. That way you will get the most recent information available. Next, you should look at the various types of BK.

There are business and nonbusiness, voluntary and involuntary bankruptcies. Chapter 7 is liquidation of nonexempt assets of businesses or individuals. Chapter 9 is an adjustment of debts of a municipal government. Chapter 11 is reorganization for businesses or individuals. Chapter 12 is an adjustment of debts for a family farmer with regular income. Chapter 13 is an adjustment of debts of an individual with regular income. Let's look at a few of the options the average consumer could use.

Chapter Thirteen Bankruptcy

Chapter 13 BK is part of a federal law enacted by Congress to help people with bad financial problems. A Chapter 13 agreement is a method for individuals, and small business owners who are experiencing financial difficulties to pay their debts over a specified time. The plan allows the person or business owing the debts to make reduced payments budgeted to fit their income and expenses. Usually, the payments are manageable.

The Chapter 13 participant makes payments to the person who serves as trustee for the bankruptcy court. The Chapter 13 trustee supervises and administers all the agreements within his or her district. The trustee supervises and maintains accurate records, makes payment to the creditors, and can help with the problems that arise in making the agreement a workable plan.

There is a fee charged by the BK court for filing a Chapter 13 plan. A BK attorney or the BK court can tell you the current fee. It will not be a very large sum of money. The BK court will supervise your payments to your creditors. Usually, the plan allows for reasonable payments over a period of time. Through this plan, you will receive enough income for your personal needs. You will have enough money left over to afford a decent standard of living. However, you will probably not live a lifestyle of the rich and famous.

Some experts believe that Chapter 13 is the answer! In his book, *Ten Cents On The Dollar* (Simon & Schuster, NY), author Sidney Ruthberg mentions important information. "Some bankruptcy experts think Chapter XIII is just plain dumb, and in New York, where you find the most sophisticated bankruptcy people, you see very few XIII's. Why beat your brains out to pay off a lot of debts if you can get your debts expunged forever by getting a discharge in bankruptcy?"

Yes, why would anyone want to live with something hanging over them for three to five years, when it could be over in six months? Again, there must be something, some psychological quirk in people's minds, about the American work ethic. Work hard, pay your bills, obey the law, etc. Some people believe they will feel better if they pay off the BK plan. Well, usually a little antacid could help!

In the past, people called Chapter 13 "The Wage Earner's Plan." Now, officially, the title is "Adjustments of Debts of an Individual with Regular Income." However, most everyone calls it Chapter 13. (Remember, regardless of where you live within the United States, you live within a bankruptcy court's jurisdiction.) The main consideration in a Chapter 13 plan approval is income. Your income must be sufficient to provide for regular payments to the trustee, during the time specified by the plan.

This time can range from three years (usually) on up to five years. If your income is irregular, you might not be eligible for Chapter 13 consideration. If you have no income, you will not be eligible for benefits under Chapter 13. You might want to consider other sections of the bankruptcy law, such as Chapter 7.

A prime benefit of Chapter 13 is that it places all your creditors on "hold" or "timeout." Chapter 13 stops wage attachments and associated contact by your creditors. Also, Chapter 13 stops late charges and service charges, and frequently stops interest accumulation on your past due accounts. Chapter 13 also stops repossessions and foreclosures. Chapter 13 protects any co-signers you may have. Chapter 13 can protect some of your savings, if you have any left. Also, Chapter 13 can protect part of the equity in your home, if you still own one.

People in certain occupations cannot participate in a Chapter 13 plan. Stock brokers and commodity brokers cannot use Chapter 13 BK. However, nearly everyone who has regular income can apply for Chapter 13. Income can come from wages, self-employment, or a profession. Also, you must have unsecured debts less than $100,000 and secured debts less than $350,000.

A "sole proprietorship" must produce enough income to cover current expenses. Those include your household budget and expenses within your business. There must be enough income available to pay the planned payments, based on debts you got before you filed Chapter 13. The BK court may require the business to file monthly statements. Those could include cash receipts and disbursements, profit and loss statements, current balance sheet, and a report of the taxes that are due and payable.

When considering Chapter 13, an attorney will ask you about your salary and debts. Based on your income and existing debts, can you pay off all your creditors in four months? If you cannot pay your old debts in that time, you may want to consider Chapter 13. That may be a good alternative to your present situation.

Also, many attorneys may ask for a comparison of four times your salary and wages to the total debt you owe. If Bob Smith earned

$1,250 each month, multiplied by four, there is a base figure of $5,000. This means if Bob Smith's debts were above $5,000, he should consider protection under Chapter 13.

Chapter 13 may not be the complete answer to your problems, but it will allow you a little breathing room. You must examine the living habits that got you so far into debt in the first place. You simply cannot continue to live the way you lived in the past. Chapter 13 means a serious belt-tightening period that can last from three to five years.

Are you prepared, mentally-physically-financially, for three to five years of constantly being alert to your financial situation? Will you have a steady job and enough income? There are many unknowns you must consider. You must prepare yourself to succeed with a Chapter 13 BK plan.

Another benefit of Chapter 13 is flexibility. The BK court has the right to increase or reduce your payments if there is an unforeseen change in your income. Such a change may be an increase or decrease in your wages.

What if you had a plan approved for three years, made all the required payments, and still owed a balance? The BK court might discharge the balance of debts, rather than extend the plan.

Also, Chapter 13 allows for negotiation. Say, for instance, that you purchased a bedroom set for $1,200 and still owe $950. The actual value of the merchandise could be as little as $250. The physical merchandise — the bedroom set — secures the purchase or loan. Through negotiation, you could have the debt set at $250 plus a percentage of the balance owed. This would reduce the amount owed by half or more in some cases.

If you purchase a television set for $500 and still owe $300, the retailer may agree on a lower amount. This is due to the cost to the retailer of picking up the item and preparing it to be resold. Often, a retailer will accept a lower price through the Chapter 13 plan. The retailer may not want to bother with the costs of repossession and resale.

A Chapter 13 trustee is duty bound to discover all your assets. The trustee could take any property of any value that is not exempt. To find out about exemptions in your state, you need to visit a law library or a public library. Legal encyclopedias of your state laws will contain the information you need. Use the index and look up "exemptions."

Upon examining this section, you can write down the exemptions that apply to your situation. This will give you a clear idea of *what not to have on hand* if you decide to file for Chapter 13 or 7 bankruptcy.

Another benefit of Chapter 13 concerns your credit rating. If you have to file a Chapter 13 or Chapter 7 BK, chances are your credit already is in the toilet. During your Chapter 13 plan, it might be difficult to get new credit. However, if you successfully complete the Chapter 13 plan, many creditors will look upon that as something good. That is, you paid the debts, although you had to pay through a Chapter 13 plan trustee. Some creditors might be willing to extend you credit, knowing that you stuck it out and paid off your agreed upon debt.

On the other hand, the situation is different if you filed straight BK or "general discharge." If the court allows a final discharge of your debts, most creditors will not accept you as creditworthy. However, some creditors may view you as a good credit risk. Most creditors know you cannot file for BK again within six years.

You must remember what got you into the mess in the first place. There are ways to rebuild your credit, gradually and with due caution, of course. (More on this in another chapter.)

A final benefit of Chapter 13 concerns failure of the plan. If your Chapter 13 plan fails, regardless of the reason, you can go ahead and file for complete bankruptcy. What happens if you are two years into a four year Chapter 13 plan, and you lose your job? If you do not find another job quickly, there will be a problem. You must keep up reasonable payments to the Chapter 13 plan. If you cannot make the payments, you might have to file a Chapter 7 BK.

Chapter 7 Bankruptcy

Chapter 7 BK is also known as "general bankruptcy," "general discharge," or "straight bankruptcy." Under this BK, you admit that it is not possible to pay your debts. You will ask the court to declare you bankrupt. This, in effect, dismisses nearly all of your debts.

When you file for Chapter 7, the court appoints a trustee to supervise or administer your case. Again, this trustee will look for anything of value that he or she can attach or sell — items that are not exempt. "Harvesting assets" helps the trustee, and the creditors listed on your bankruptcy petition.

If you have been out of work for a while, you have probably sold most anything of value, to pay your rent or buy groceries. It is very possible that your remaining property will fall into the exempt class. If you have very little personal property, cash, equity in real estate, etc., your case will probably be a *"no assets"* case.

A no assets case simply tells the creditors there are no assets left. Also, "no assets" means the creditors have little chance to recover any money. In a no assets case, there is very little harassment and few legal complications for the debtor. Once you let everyone know the cash register is empty, almost everyone leaves you alone. Of course, the trustee still has to make sure you have no saleable assets.

In the true tradition of detectives, most trustees will examine your circumstances and lifestyle very carefully. If the trustee finds some assets you did not declare, or that you transferred property before filing BK, you will be in a lot of trouble. It is best to come clean, rather than risk the wrath of a federal BK Judge! Plus, you may risk having the remainder of the legal system wanting to take care of you. Also, an intentional fraud in court will get your BK discharge reversed! Hiding any assets is not worth one day in prison.

The BK proceedings involving the Smiths was a Chapter 7, no assets case. The Smiths had to appear at a "first meeting of creditors." During this meeting, creditors were present to ask questions of the Smiths. Often, this meeting of creditors does not have a judge present. Instead, the judge may send a representative from the court. This person acts for the judge.

Under oath, Bob and Mariela Smith had to answer all questions presented by the creditors. In the Smith case, of the several creditors present, only one creditor asked any questions. The creditor asked whether or not the Smith family still had certain merchandise. The Smiths replied they had sold the merchandise some time ago, so they could buy food. Bob Smith later learned that merchandise would normally fall into the exempt class. The creditor could not repossess that merchandise.

Although the Smith car had clear title for a few years, the Smiths took out a small loan against the car. They owed $450 on that loan, using the car as security. The Smiths "reaffirmed" this debt. That means they were willing to continue making payments on the loan. The collection officer at the bank was a pleasant, helpful person. Therefore, the Smiths made no effort to renegotiate the loan to a smaller balance. (Some people will renegotiate the balance owed, to try to obtain a smaller balance.)

Had the Smiths not reaffirmed the loan, the bank would have repossessed the car. Then the bank would have sold the car for whatever they could get, usually at auction. Also, the bank might have consigned the car to a company that specializes in selling or auctioning bank repossessions.

However, repossessing a car and reselling it to pay off a loan can be *very expensive* for a bank. An exception is a car that is nearly brand new or highly valuable. If the bank cannot profit from the repossession, they will usually pass up the opportunity to repossess the car.

Many months later, the Smiths made their final payment on the loan secured by their car. Then the bank informed the local credit bureau the payments were complete, as promised, or "as agreed." That statement could be a possible future credit reference!

If you decide not to reaffirm a co-signed note, that could add up to trouble for the co-signer. The court will discharge your debt. *HOWEVER, whoever co-signed the note might get stuck with having to pay off the loan!* That can lead to hostility between the co-signer and you. For that reason, most BK attorneys require you to list the note co-signer as a creditor within the BK proceedings.

Chapter 13 and Chapter 7 BK forms are almost standard throughout the country, although various publishing companies print the forms. Two of the printers are Julius Blumberg, Incorporated, and Graham-Pierce Legal Printers. Prices for these forms will vary, depending on where you buy them. Usually, the forms have a cover sheet that you remove and use as a work sheet. You must type the actual forms and use carbon copies.

In the forms for Chapter 7 BK, the first sheet is the title page, VOLUNTARY CASE: DEBTOR'S JOINT PETITION. This form lists your name and address, telephone number, Social Security number, the date and your signature. The next page is STATEMENT OF FINANCIAL AFFAIRS FOR DEBTOR NOT ENGAGED IN BUSINESS. This involves two pages and about 15 questions. The questions deal with your names and addresses of past years. Also, the forms ask about your finances for the past six years. The forms also ask where you have filed tax returns and where you have savings and checking accounts, etc.

The next section is SCHEDULES OF ASSETS AND LIABILITIES. Schedule A, Statement of All Liabilities of Debtor, Schedule A-1, asks you to list creditors having priority. These include wages owed to workers and contributions to employee benefit plans. Also included are any deposits for certain items you did not deliver, and taxes owed to various taxing authorities.

The next page is Schedule A-2, Creditors Holding Security. This form asks you to list all your secured debts. The Smiths' car was a secured debt. A home you are buying, secured by any type of loan, is a secured debt, etc.

Schedule A-3, Creditors Having Unsecured Claims Without Priority, asks you to list all your unsecured creditors. Here you must list ALL credit collection agencies connected with you in any way. You could owe a debt to a retail store. That store could have assigned or sold your account to a collection firm. That firm might have sold the collection account to another collection firm, or an attorney, etc. One retail debt could have several collection firms associated with it. *YOU MUST LIST ALL OF THEM.*

Next is Schedule B, Statement of All Property of Debtor. Schedule B-1, Real Property, asks you to list all your real property. This means real estate. You must include land, the vacation cabin, the second home in Malibu, the home you are buying now, etc.

Schedule B-2, Personal Property, asks you to list all your personal property and the market value of such. Usually, you should list any items that have any significant value. Next is Schedule B-3, Property Not Otherwise Scheduled. This asks you to list property transferred under assignment for benefit of creditors within 120 days before filing the BK petition. Also, you must list all property of any kind not otherwise scheduled.

The next page is Schedule B-4, Property Claimed as Exempt. On this page, you list all the property the court allows you to claim as exempt. Also, you must list the location of the property. Then you must refer to the statute creating the exemption, and the value of the items claimed as exempt. The next page is a Summary of Debts and Property. On this page, you enter the total of the previous schedules. You list your various debts and all your assets. You must show this as a dollar figure, totaled from the various pages where you listed your property. This page lists the total of the debts found in the A Schedules and the property listed in the B Schedules. At the bottom of the page, there is a "Declaration." Under the penalty of perjury, you swear or affirm that the information is true and correct. The court will probably require you to provide a mailing label sheet with all your creditors (and collection folks) listed. You do this so the court can mail the required notices concerning your petition for BK. There are specific guide sheets required, and you will have to find out what your local BK court requires.

The court uses this master sheet to make pressure-sensitive labels. Normally, the court will mail many letters concerning your case. So it is very important to have the correct form and to list the complete name, mailing address, and zip code of each creditor.

You may want to use a guide book or information packet about doing a BK by yourself. Otherwise, you may have some difficulty completing these forms. However, an authoritative book on how to do self BK will show you how to complete the forms. After you have completed the work sheets, you could hire an attorney to check the forms for completeness and accuracy. If that attorney who specializes in BK approves your forms, you send or deliver the forms to the court. Within a few days, the court will respond, telling you the filing fee for the initiation of BK action.

The court has some compassion about personal financial difficulties. If the filing fee is too much for you to come up with all at one time, the court may let you pay the filing fee in installments. However, you must pay the filing fee in full, before the first meeting of creditors. THIS IS ONE BILL YOU WANT TO PAY ON TIME! The Smiths made three payments, as approved by the court.

About 90 to 120 days after your first meeting of creditors, the court will mail a notice of a final discharge hearing. This notice goes to you and all your creditors. Customarily, the judge makes an appearance at this meeting. This should be your second and final required court appearance. At this hearing, the judge will either approve or deny your BK petition. Also, the judge will approve any reaffirmations you agreed to sign. A few days later, you will receive a formal document called Final Discharge Order in the mail. This is a court document discharging your debts.

**OUTSTANDING
INSTALLMENT
DEBT
IN BILLIONS**

**1988—663.0
1989—724.4
1990—738.8
1991—735.5
1992—741.1**
Source: 113th Edition
Statistical Abstract of
The United States,
1993

Figure 4

The Chapter 7 BK can remain in your credit record for up to ten years. Once the court grants final approval of your petition under Chapter 7, you cannot file another Chapter 7 for six years. However, BK laws will permit you to file for Chapter 13, if you need to do that. After Chapter 7 discharge of your debts, it might be very difficult to get credit. By following the example of the Smiths, you could build some credit. Remember to be honest with the credit manager at the store where you need the credit.

The main opportunity extended through Chapter 7 BK is a *FRESH START*. Remember, once the court grants discharge of your debts, you will have a fresh start. How you choose to take advantage of the fresh start will determine your success or failure in the future. As soon as you get a new job, you can start building toward a better standard of living.

There is a terrible lesson to learn by having to file for Chapter 13 or Chapter 7 bankruptcy. The lesson is to look at the past and learn how you spent beyond your means. I'd wager that most consumer BKs are a direct result of major overspending through the credit card system.

The credit card system continually urges people to spend "money" they do not have. It is so easy to fall into the trap. Once you are in the hole, it is very, very difficult to climb out of it. In the last few years, many millions of people have filed for protection under the U.S. bankruptcy laws. There are millions of people who experienced receiving credit, credit failure, and personal financial failure. Most of these people will probably be very careful about credit and over-extending themselves in the future.

Look at the table of BK filings over the last few years (Figure 3, page 18).

You must use your fresh start wisely. Otherwise, it will not take very long before you are in financial trouble again. There are many firms across the nation that will help you get a new VISA or MasterCard. Normally, you will pay the firm an application fee (up front fee) of about $25. Once the card company or bank accepts you, they will ask you to place a deposit into a savings account. The amounts required vary and some start at $250. PRESTO, you have a credit card with a restricted charging limit. The amount you can charge is roughly half of your deposit. Such a card will allow you to rent a car or sleep in a good hotel. Here is a partial list of companies that offer secured credit cards. Some banks offer a nation-wide program, others offer the program only to residents in that state. You can call during regular business hours, and get information about the requirements of these card companies. These represent a random selection, with no preference intended.

First Deposit National Bank, 1-800-356-0107
American Pacific Bank, 1-800-879-8745
Bank One, 1-800-395-2555
Citibank, 1-800-743-1332
Signet Bank, 1-800-333-7116
Texas Bank, 1-800-451-0273
Central National Bank of Mattoon, 1-800-876-9119
Sterling Bank, 1-800-763-2265

Even with this type of credit card, you have to be careful. It is very easy to fall back into the hole once you are out on level ground. My hope is that by reading this book, you will learn something about what goes on within the credit system. Also, I want you to know where to get help if you need it. I want you to know the type of help available to you. I want you to know when to use the help. Most importantly, you need to know how to go about *Ditching Your Debts*, if you have to do that.

5
The Small Business

"Drive thy business, or it will drive thee."
— Benjamin Franklin

The average small business springs forth from a person's desire to work for herself or himself. Sometimes this takes the form of buying an existing business. Other times, it means starting a business from scratch. The cash investment can vary from a small amount to a large sum of money.

According to the Small Business Administration, most business failures are due to inept business management. However, I believe most business failures are due to money. Lack of money to start and sustain the business must be the major cause of business failure.

Many business advisers will recommend that you have at least six months of operating capital. Preferably, you should have at least one year of operating capital in the bank. That means you should have six to twelve months of your expenses covered by a deposit in the bank. Start up costs, utilities, rent, payroll, insurance and other major costs need to be on deposit in the bank.

You need this type of protection when you start new or adjust an existing business. Many people entering business on their own have an attitude of, "I can make it," or, "That will not happen to me." Most of these people overlook the requirement for a very large cash reserve. That is why so many small businesses fail.

Anyone can walk around the average small or large town and see evidence of businesses having a tough time. The sure sign of this problem is the attempt to sell something at practically any price. Thus, you will see signs in windows announcing 50% off everything. Some stores will have discounts of 70% or more. Not every business that advertises a store-wide clearance is having financial troubles. However, many are. Turnover in shopping malls is another benchmark sign of a bad economy.

Most business failures will involve a sole proprietorship. There are three basic forms of business ownership. These are Sole Proprietorship, Partnership and Corporation. The sole proprietorship is the only type of business specifically designed for operation by one person. However, it is possible to have a corporation owned and operated by one person.

Sometimes the sole proprietorship is a husband and wife team. Usually, only one of them will be the "owner" of the business. However, some states now recognize a husband and wife as a sole proprietor.

In the sole proprietorship, the owner is his or her own supervisor and works for him- or herself. The owner enjoys the profits brought about by his or her own hard work. The owner of the sole proprietorship also might see the failure of the business. If the business fails, the family could fail as well.

If a person's income comes from a business they operate, the business must prosper. If the business does not do well, the family will suffer along with the business. It is like getting a layoff notice while the factory is slow. In short, if there are no sales, there is no family income. That is why it is so important to have a large reserve in the bank. The staying power of the cash reserve will be like a life jacket, for use in times of emergency.

The main ingredient in a successful business operation is location. You can have an outstanding product, a marginal location, and no business. On the other hand, you can have a business where people will seek you out because of your reputation. Most retail-oriented businesses are very dependent on foot traffic. If you have a service business, location is not as important.

With the good location, you must have a top quality accounting system. You would not believe how many businesses do their books once a year, around the tax filing deadline. You should have a monthly bookkeeper. Sure, this can be costly. However, you should know where you are, financially, from month to month. Even a quarterly system is better than once a year.

Daily, you should record your sales, or income, and your expenses. Once a month, it is very easy to add up the various sales and expenses. You do not have to be an accountant or bookkeeper to do this. Normally, if you provide totaled figures to your accountant or bookkeeper, they will charge less for their services. If the accountant or bookkeeper has to go through a large bag or box stuffed with papers, that fee will be higher. If you provide accurate information, you will get fast, accurate bookkeeping statements.

There are hundreds of books written about small business management. I cannot possibly tell you all about small business management in this short space. However, you need to know about the major problem areas facing small business owners. The small business owner dealing with slow business faces the same problems as an unemployed person. There is a direct parallel leading to financial ruin, if both are not careful.

With a small business, the money, location and record keeping challenges are similar to a person trying to survive in a job for wages. Major problems in any of those areas can mean difficulty for the small business owner. Combined problems from those areas will probably cause failure of the small business enterprise.

Here is some advice about going into small business: Keep your eyes and ears open. Do not be fooled by the apparent simplicity of the business. Most small businesses are deceptively difficult to operate successfully. Make sure you have the cash reserves for staying power. Be very certain about the location you select. If you have doubts about anything, seek the advice of an expert. Pay the price for the expert's opinion and avoid financial ruin later. Make sure your accounting methods are the best available. With enough money, a good location, and responsible accounting, the rest is up to you and your products or services. Remember that word of mouth advertising can lead your business toward failure or success.

Anyone wanting to ditch debts or get lost needs to consider as many alternatives as possible. Going into business might be one of those alternatives. You can do research by yourself. If you start with your local library, you will be on track. There is a wealth of information at the library, and it is free.

Also, the Consumer Information Center has a great deal of information available. Sometimes this information is free, sometimes there is a charge. The Summer 1994 catalog had the following headings: Cars, Children-Learning activities, Children-Parenting, Employment, Federal Programs, Benefits, Food & Nutrition, Health, Drugs & Health Aids, Medical Problems, Mental Health, Housing-Buying and Financing, Housing-Home Improvements & Safety, Money-Credit, Money-Financial Planning, Small Business, Travel & Hobbies, Miscellaneous.

There are more than 200 titles. About half of the titles are free. The other half range from fifty cents to four dollars. Publications run from a few pages to 87 pages. The booklets are 15 to 65 pages. To find out what is currently available, write for the catalog. (Consumer Information Center, P.O. Box 100, Pueblo, CO, 81002.)

The Small Business Administration may help you. You can write and ask for information. You can check with your local library to find out about the SBA office nearest you. The SBA has pamphlets covering a wide range of business types. Most of the information is general in nature. If you need in-depth information, go to your library and do more research about the specific topic.

The SBA does guarantee loans made by banks to small businesses. Also, the SBA may make a direct loan if you were unable to obtain a loan from a bank. However, these loans are not easy to get. Everything concerning your business must be ready for inspection. Your bookkeeping procedures and creditworthiness must be perfect. The loan application requires a close review and verification of many items.

Many people believe the SBA hands out loans freely to anyone who asks. That is not the case. In past years, there was evidence of political favoritism. If you needed a business loan and knew someone who knew someone, you could get a loan. The political corruption scandals forced many government agencies to change their methods of doing business. Now there is talk of doing away with or consolidating many government agencies, including the SBA.

What if the person wanting to ditch debts or get lost is now in business? It might not be too late to contact the people from S.C.O.R.E., the Service Core of Retired Executives. Write or call the nearest S.B.A. office and tell them you need to speak with someone from S.C.O.R.E. Also, your local library may have the contact information for local S.C.O.R.E. participants.

The Service Corps of Retired Executives has many retired experts on call to help the small business owner. They do not lend money. They do examine your circumstance and provide advice or recommendations. S.C.O.R.E. advisers are "retired" people who have business experience. They usually have many years of business management experience with larger companies. Many of these people are experts in their field, be it advertising, accounting, purchasing, etc.

The person from S.C.O.R.E will be honest with you. If your situation looks so bad you should "fold up the tent," they will suggest you consider that. On the other hand, if practical business methods will help your situation, they will be as quick to make those recommendations.

Local banks could be a source of information. Some banks prepare informational pamphlets or newsletters that cover a wide variety of topics. Some topics might include economic conditions and information of interest to small business owners. There could be an article by the bank's chief economist. Such an article may discuss past and future business activities in your region. There could be advice that may help the small business owner.

Most banks and libraries subscribe to local papers and *The Wall Street Journal*. To get information about how to subscribe to *The Wall Street Journal,* call 1-800-JOURNAL. You could make more informed choices by reading several business publications. To inquire about a subscription to *California Business,* call 1-415-776-9966. Remember, business management principles and concepts apply to both small and large businesses. Again, your local library may have several publications you can read for free.

Business publications cannot solve your present business problems overnight. However, you could save time or money with what you will learn. By staying informed, you may gain the competitive edge necessary to survive and succeed. If your small business makes it past one year, it could be a good sign of future success.

However, most business problems crop up in the second or third year of business operation. Once your business makes it past five years, there is an excellent chance it will survive. That is why it is so important to have the financial "staying power" mentioned earlier. That six to twelve month operating expense cash reserve should stay in the bank as long as you own the business. From time to time, you should add to the cash reserve until you have about three years of staying power.

No one can predict disasters or bad economic times with any certainty. You can never tell when something might happen that could have a harmful effect on your business. If something bad happens, you will not mind having that money in the bank, waiting to help you. Also, you might need to borrow money from the bank. Then you can use your staying power deposit as collateral. This will allow you to borrow money without having to use your savings.

One topic often neglected by the small business owner is the *business plan.* Most experts agree that a business plan is essential to the success of any business. Do you think large corporations conduct their activities without a business plan? Not very likely! Some small businesses operate successfully without a business plan. However, all businesses should put their goals into a written plan. Reviewing this plan is like looking at a road map. It can show you where you have been, where you are, and what is ahead of you.

The business plan is a simple matter of stating your goals and what you plan to do to achieve them. Writing down your goals and how you plan to meet those goals will provide you with a course of action. The plan will serve as a constant reminder of what you need to do. Without a business plan, it is too easy to stray from your original goals. The defined business plan will keep you on the path to success.

Of course, good decisions come from having two or more alternatives. You should have several alternatives to choose from whenever you need to decide a course of action. By looking at several options, you can choose a correct course of action. You should have a plan with primary and secondary goals. Remember, it is OK to copy the "formula for success" enjoyed by other businesses. Management that is successful for someone else might also help you succeed.

Remember, if your business begins to fail, it can take you with it. If you borrow money to keep your business going, you might be getting deeper into the quicksand. An unsecured loan is not easy to get. That is a loan based on the creditworthiness of you and your business. A secured loan will require equipment or property as collateral. Many small business owners try to keep their business going by borrowing against their home. This could be a big mistake. If your business is failing, you should consider letting it do just that... as early as possible. The longer you wait, the worse it will be. No business is worth having your health and savings drained.

6

Making Decisions

"What we have to learn to do we learn by doing."
— Aristotle

I do not know who the author is, but there is a saying I remember from many years ago. I will try to paraphrase it as best as I can:

Reasonably intelligent men, when in the presence of facts, and with common objectives in mind, should not have too much trouble coming into agreement.

Most people will agree with this statement. When you need to decide something, you need the facts and a goal. Many people firmly believe that good decisions come from two or more alternatives. People credit Benjamin Franklin as the person who originated the "T Decision Maker," or decision matrix.

To use this "T" decision maker, you get a piece of paper. Then you make a large letter T at the top of the paper. On top of the T, write your problem requiring an answer. Should I move? Should I change my job? Should I buy a certain product? Then you list the bad points on one side and the good points on the other side. Whichever side has the most entries will serve as a guide to action. For an example, see Figure 5.

You can see that it is simple to list the good and bad points, and then make a comparison. Of course, this type of decision matrix may not apply in all situations. But it can help you most of the time. The main benefit of the decision matrix is the elimination of emotional responses in making a choice. By carefully evaluating what you decide are good or bad points, you can help keep emotions out of the decision.

People can use this decision making process for many situations. You can use the "'T'" for something as simple as a buying decision. Also, you can use the "'T" to help decide something as complicated as changing a relationship.

Should I Move From My Present House?	
Present House	**House in New Area**
rent is $450	rent is $550
plumbing is bad	house in good shape
roof leaks in bed-room	large fenced yard
rent increase soon	has fireplace
no fireplace	three bedrooms
two bedrooms	insulated
expensive to heat	moderate heat bills
landlord is a jerk	landlord seems ok
	bigger kitchen
	has new carpet
	freshly painted
	closer to work

Figure 5

7

The Second Mortgage Trap

Many people believe the answer to the question, "How do you spell relief?", is S-E-C-O-N-D — M-O-R-T-G-A-G-E! Yes, a second or third mortgage may bring relief. However, the relief is usually temporary, as in the example of the Smiths.

For example, suppose you purchased a home for $100,000 and you owe a balance of $80,000. Based on recent sales of similar homes within your neighborhood, you believe your home might be worth approximately $130,000. Your possible equity is around $50,000. You could borrow up to about $24,000. You could receive cash in that amount, less costs.

If your home appraised at $130,000, some lenders will let you borrow 80% of the appraised amount. A few lenders might go higher than 80% loan-to-value. Eighty percent of $130,000 is $104,000. From the $104,000 you take away what you owe on the first mortgage, $80,000. That leaves you with $24,000. It sounds good to have $24,000, right? *WRONG!* While you can get a loan for $24,000, your net proceeds will be much smaller.

First, the loan company charges a variety of fees for making this loan. There are processing fees, document fees, etc., in addition to "points." Plus, there are numerous other fees charged through the title and escrow part of the transaction. Those companies charge for their work on the loan. They must coordinate a flow of information and paper between the lender and the borrower.

Also, there will be interest charges for part of the month when you make the loan. In short, it costs a lot to borrow on a second or third mortgage. It is possible to pay no points when making a second mortgage. However, the borrower could face from two points to fifteen or more points. Each point is one percent of the loan amount.

It is not very easy to show an average cost of a second mortgage. That is due to each loan having its own circumstances. Most lenders charge loan fees and points, based on the amount of risk involved. If you have marginal credit, you are going to pay higher everything.

Lenders grade credit like teachers grade students' work. If you have perfect credit, income, and job stability, you are "A" credit risk. From there, it goes to A-, B+, and so on, to F credit. An example of F credit is someone who is in active BK or foreclosure, and has mostly bad credit. That means 60 to 90 days late on most of their consumer credit bills and loans. It also can mean someone who has one or more notices of default, or "NOD," filed against their property. A lender files NOD when you fall 30 days or more behind in your payments.

Most lenders who specialize in making second or third mortgages also specialize in taking advantage of people. Yes, they insist they are providing a needed service, but at what cost? Often, people who can afford it the least fall victim to high loan costs. Total loan costs (interest, brokerage and/or lender fees, and other costs) can approximate 25% to 50% of the loan amount.

In 1985, an average interest rate for a second mortgage was 17%. In 1988, the interest rates for second mortgages ranged from 11% to 15%. In 1994, the interest rate for a second mortgage, arranged through private money, was about 13%. A second mortgage for $24,000 at 13%, interest only, has payments of $260 per month.

The longer you keep the mortgage, the more expensive it is. In 24 months, you will pay $6,240. In 60 months, you will pay $15,600. Remember, those payments are "rent payments." At the end of 24 or 60 months, you still owe $24,000.

Brokerage points could range from one to 15 or more. For this example I will use 8 points. Eight percent of $24,000 is $1,920. Other loan costs such as appraisal, title insurance, escrow fee, prepaid interest, recording fee, notary fee, etc. could easily cost another $2,000 or more. So, the cost of your loan for one year is $7,040. This is the total of monthly interest payments, points, and other costs. $260 X 12 = $3,120, plus, $1,920, plus $2,000. Divide $7,040 by $24,000 and you get 29.3%. The second year, your total loan cost is $10,160. Divide that by $24,000 and you get 42.3%. You can see how the cost of keeping this loan adds up very fast.

One of the major scams by some of the mortgage banks and companies is credit life insurance. The premium fee can start at $300 to $400 and go much higher. Usually, it is an obscure insurance company that provides the coverage. The premium costs the mortgage bank or company very little. Therefore, this life insurance is a major "profit center" for them.

This is another clever way for lenders to "harvest dollars" from people who cannot afford it. Of course, the lender conveniently adds the credit life insurance fee to your loan costs. The main business philosophy is to have you spend money on paper. That makes it more painless. Most borrowers focus their interest on the bottom line. That is, how much money will they get? Therefore, costs become a blur. Someone desperate for the money will not pay close attention to the costs.

If you need this type of loan, go to a full-service bank or similar lending institution first. There, you may be able to find more favorable lending conditions. A regular bank, savings and loan, or mortgage bank, may have lower loan fees and a better interest rate. However, these lenders may have certain requirements you will have to meet. For example, they may require employment and income at a certain level. Also the bank may restrict how much they will lend, based on your credit report information. Most lenders require the verification of many items before the application will go to an underwriter.

On the other hand, private money investors may be more lenient. Usually, mortgage brokers represent private investors. However, some private investors make their own loans. With this type of lending, employment and income are not as important. Most private lenders focus on the equity in your home. As long as you are alive and have enough equity, there will probably be a private lender for your situation. Their main concern is the safety of their money.

Most of these lenders do not want to take a home in foreclosure. However, some private lenders have foreclosure as their main goal. If you do not make the payments, the lender will foreclose on your property. Foreclosure is the legal process for lenders to take possession of your home. It is a process that can take up to several months. However, certain types of foreclosure can happen very quickly. The federal bankruptcy court is about the only entity that can stop a foreclosure. If you face foreclosure, you need to consider BK quickly. You will want to do this to protect any remaining equity.

Not all borrowers use second mortgage money to add onto their home. The second mortgage firms advertise that you can take out a homeowner's equity loan and spend it on anything. You could have the cash for a vacation, new car, pay your bills, etc. These second mortgage loan companies try to make it look like you are crazy if you do not take out a second mortgage or "equity loan." These lenders use slick advertising and many people fall for it. Nowadays, the high risk is an "equity line of credit." The lender provides a line of credit secured by a second deed of trust on your home. This sounds fashionable, but can be a costly mistake.

Many of these loans are adjustable loans with high lifetime cap rates, or no cap rates at all. Also, most of these adjustable loans have a very high margin. That is the adjustment factor for setting the new interest rate at certain intervals. Anything over a margin of 250 is high. Many second mortgages and equity lines of credit have margins of 350, 450, and as high as 650. A higher margin assures the lender of maximum interest rate increases at each adjustment. If it is a negative amortization type loan, high margin will add deferred interest to your principal balance. You could borrow $50,000 and end up owing $62,000!

If you need to get such a loan, you could end up in more trouble than when you started. Only this time, you risk losing your home. Your situation could improve for awhile. A loan will allow you to catch up on your bills, spend some money on items you need or want, and otherwise have a good time. However, those good times can disappear fast!

For example, your first mortgage has principal, interest, taxes and insurance payments of $550 per month. Then you get a second mortgage of $50,000 at 14%, interest only. This will add $583.33 to your present housing expense. Your new monthly total will be $1,133.88. This might not be very easy for you to handle. The credit cards you vowed you would never use again might start to call your name. All of those unused high credit limits, with current zero balances, serve as a constant encouragement to spend. You should close your accounts and cut up your cards, etc. If not, you could be in serious trouble within as little as three months after catching up on your debts! That is **THE SECOND MORTGAGE TRAP.**

Getting out of the trap can be very expensive. The best solution is preventive. *DO NOT* go for a second mortgage. The bankruptcy laws allow you to keep a certain portion of your equity. You could be better off, and financially ahead, by going through bankruptcy. This will allow you to make sure that your court allowed equity is exempt. If you sell your home immediately before filing BK, make sure you place your equity in exempt investments or goods.

If you find yourself considering a second mortgage, try to get a *refinance loan* instead. If your credit is still good, most lenders will consider you for a "refi loan." Most lenders will allow you to have cash back, up to 75% or 80% of the appraised value. For example, you owe $88,000 on your home. The appraised value is $168,000. Multiply $168,000 by 80% and you get $134,400. Subtract $88,000 from $134,400 and you get $46,400. That is your equity, the $46,400. Instead of getting a second mortgage for that amount, the lender will provide you with a new loan of $134,400.

Present rates in 1994, are about 9.5% for a 30-year fixed-rate loan. Your principal and interest payments on $134,400 will be about $1,034. If your existing loan was $90,000 at 8.25%, the principal and interest payments would be $677. If you get a second mortgage of $46,400 at 14.0%, the interest payment will be $541. The total of the first and second will be $1,218. Therefore, a refi loan will give you higher payments, but lower than the first and second combined. In this example, the refi loan will save about $184 per month, compared to the first and second. Plus, your total loan costs should be lower with the refi loan than with the second mortgage.

Remember, most second mortgages of B+ through D- credit, do not fully amortize. Usually, second and third mortgages are interest only. The payments are monthly, for a defined number of months. Your last payment is the interest, plus the principal. In the above example of $46,400, you have interest only monthly payments of $541.

If your loan is for 36 months, the payments will total $19,476 plus the last payment of $46,400. Unless you have the cash, you will have to get another loan. This is precisely what the mortgage companies hope will happen to you. Usually, they will "extend" the loan, for the payment of an extension fee. Sometimes you pay this fee in cash; other times, they add it to the loan balance.

It is far better to have a loan that *fully amortizes*. That means there will be no balance at the end of your loan term. Remember, be cautious when getting any type of mortgage. If you have bad credit, you will have to pay the going rate.

Homesteading Your Property

Most states allow for the protection of a family home. Sometimes, the home and up to about 160 acres of adjoining land can have protection, if you have filed a *"Homestead Declaration."* You must file this declaration with the appropriate government agencies.

If you are buying your home and are in a bad financial situation, you should consider filing a homestead declaration.

Usually, this document is simple to complete. It is a document that states your home is your chief place of residency. Further, you declare it to be your homestead. After that, you record the document with the proper local government agencies where people record land transactions.

You can buy the form from most stationery stores. It does not cost very much. Your local library may have information on how to complete the form. Usually, you must fill in some blank spots with your name, address and a legal description of the property. Most county recorders do not charge much for a one or two page document.

The act of homesteading your property protects part of the equity in your property.

The amount of protection will vary with the different states. It is a good idea to check the laws of your state. Again, your local library should have the information you need.

The whole point of homesteading your property is to protect your equity. If your home is worth $150,000 and you owe $100,000 against it, the difference is your *equity*. If you were to sell your home at a price of $150,000 you would receive $50,000 less costs. If you have filed a homestead declaration, most creditors will not be able to get at your $50,000 equity. Otherwise, you could be having all types of trouble with creditors and lawsuits for large amounts of money.

Only your existing mortgage and any tax liens have collection priority. They get paid before you do. Usually, creditors who have filed liens against your property will not be able to beat the homestead exemption and collect against you.

If you end up in bankruptcy, the homestead exemption will allow you to keep a certain amount of the equity in your property. You will have to consult your state bankruptcy exemptions, versus the federal exemptions, to determine which will be more favorable in your case.

Remember that homestead exemptions and bankruptcy laws vary from state to state. Probably, the most favorable state for BK is California. If your financial situation has you thinking about BK, think about California. If that state has the most favorable exemptions, you may want to move to California. Then you can declare "user friendly" BK.

8

Collection Agency Workings

"He that wants money wants everything."
— Richard Cumberland

Today, credit bureaus can use nation-wide computer information networks. You have heard of the saying, "you can run, but you cannot hide." With the average credit bureau, that saying is almost true. You should avoid these places as much as possible. There is one exception. You can check your own credit.

You can go to the nearest credit bureau and say that a department store or credit card company denied you credit. Mention that the lady you talked with suggested that you contact the credit bureau for further details. Ask to see your credit file so you can determine why they denied you credit. This is your opportunity to see what they have on you. Of course, you could actually apply for a credit card and get refused. Usually, this will allow you to review your credit without having to pay for a report.

Usually, you can examine a *copy* of your credit file. These businesses have learned over the years not to let the original file get into the hands of the person requesting a credit review. Nowadays, everything is stored in a computer anyway. Unless you are a skilled computer hacker, there is no way to alter the information.

The copy they provide you will be up-to-date and show your full credit history. You will see if they have your current address, phone number, Social Security number and employment history. *WARNING! You might have to supply such information before they will allow you to get a copy of your credit report!* Usually, for a fee, they will provide you with a copy of the report. This report will help you plan a course of action.

There could be inaccurate statements in the credit file. If so, you have the right to notify them about the mistakes and ask them to correct the mistakes. If there is any disputed information, they will allow you to tell your side of the story in 100 words or less. Sometimes, the credit bureaus are in court over the correction of errors of fact and other "misinformation."

One point to remember about credit bureaus is that they function like a vacuum. They suck up all the dirt they can. Credit bureaus go for all the information they can get. This is information provided to them by their subscribers and others who pay for credit bureau services.

Sources of information about you could include: relatives, neighbors, prospective employers, landlords, utility companies, banks, and savings & loan associations. Also, information can come from all types of insurance companies, doctors, dentists, arrest records and police reports published in local papers and legal notices. If you apply for a marriage license or business license, they know about it. If you get arrested for drunk driving, or have a judgment against you, etc., chances are the credit bureaus know about that too.

Most collection agency collectors get paid on commission or a combination of base salary plus commission. Whoever owns the account assigns the collection responsibility to the collection agency. Often, the more a collector can collect, the higher the commission or percentage they earn. Each fee arrangement is different. The collection fee might range from 25% to 75% of the money collected. Usually, the fee split is 50% of collection.

For example, say you owe $2,000 to a credit card company. You have not paid your bill, so the debt goes to a collection agency at 50% of recovery. The agency pays one of their staff, a collector, an hourly rate plus commission. The rates and commissions vary with different agencies. As an example, the agency might pay the collector $7.50 per hour and a commission of 50% of the fee earned by the agency. The collection effort could take days, weeks or months.

If the collection agency succeeds in collecting the $2,000, the agency earns $1,000. The other $1,000 goes to the card company. If the collector spent a total of six hours talking with the cardholder, and "working the case," the collector earned $45.00, the hourly rate. With the commission split, or bonus, the collector gets an additional $500. That is why bill collectors are so aggressive about you paying *anything* on the past due account.

If you have debts that are now with a collection agency, chances are a collector will work on your case with great enthusiasm for a while. If the collector keeps turning up dead leads, they will eventually lose interest in your case. Your file will go to the bottom of the stack while the collector works on more promising material. Your collection case will always be there until legally removed from the collector's jurisdiction.

However, did you know there is a time value to collection accounts? Usually, the value ranges from the point of the account being past due, to about FIVE YEARS. As each month goes by, the account becomes less valuable. Eventually, the account will be worth nothing. One past due account can go through several collection agencies. I have heard that sometimes these collection agencies buy accounts, based on the probability of collection.

Mr. Smith learned something about credit bureaus. He had a temporary job working for a retail store. His job was to help during a tax audit, by gathering information needed by the auditors. After that was done, they asked him to stay on and help with past due accounts. While he was there, Mr. Smith collected some $85,000 that was past due on purchase contracts! During this job, Mr. Smith learned that the credit collection system is not very effective in collecting money from people who have "skipped."

You could consider offering a SETTLEMENT. Let each creditor know you do not have the funds to pay the account in full. You can sincerely say how much you want to pay them the full amount. However, due to your present situation, you can only pay them 10% of the balance owed. Tell them if you file BK, they will get nothing. For example, if you have a credit card with a balance of $895, you offer them $89.50 to settle the account in full. You need to contact the card company in writing with such an offer. The card company will say yes or no. Make sure you receive their reply in writing. If they accept your offer, or make an acceptable counter offer, you must act quickly.

Get the card company to agree, in writing, to report your account paid as agreed. Also, ask them to report that information to the credit reporting agencies. Once they agree to your offer in writing, send them the amount to settle the matter. Some grocery stores offer American Express money orders for about fifty cents each. (Most banks want $3 to $5 for a money order!) The money order will provide you with a carbon copy record of the payment.

The card company may not accept your offer or make a counter offer. They may insist on the full amount. If that happens, the company will probably get aggressive about collection. Once your account goes to a collection agency, the card company may not want to discuss the matter with you. Instead, the card company will refer you to the collection agency. Sometimes the collection agency will make an offer to settle the account.

I know of a person who owed slightly more than $8,000 on one credit card. The collection agency offered to settle the account for $4,806! That is about a 40% discount. This offer had a three day time value and contained the following language. "Once said funds have been deposited, providing they are not returned by the bank, XYZABC company releases you from all claims and liabilities pertaining to your account. Furthermore, XYZABC company will inform our client of the new status of the account. In turn, our client will notify the proper credit reporting agencies." This sounds pretty good. However, it is not an agreement to report the account "paid as agreed." Also, the offer, dated March 28, 1994, required receipt of the funds by March 31, 1994. The person received the offer on the day the funds had to be deposited! Nothing like short notice! At any rate, the person did not have the money to comply.

The typical credit bureau or collection agency method of operation is to send letters requesting payment. The second, third, fourth, etc., letters become more threatening. They demand payment in full, *right now, or else!* The collection company, acting for their client, can summon you to court to get a judgment against you. If you have a job, this can end up with your wages garnisheed, or attached, to satisfy the court judgment. Usually, this is done through the court and the sheriff of the county where you reside or work.

However, if you are not working, the actions by the collection agencies amount to a constant annoyance and lots of paperwork. If you have no money or valuables, no one can expect you to come up with much in the way of settling a judgment against you. The next step, after securing a judgment against you, is to hold a creditor's examination. This is a court hearing where they will ask you all sorts of questions. There will be questions about you, your spouse, your job or lack of one, your finances, life history, etc. If, as a result of this hearing, they determine that you have some worthwhile personal property assets or real property, they may try to seize the property. They will do this in order to try to sell the property at auction. That may allow them to raise enough cash to settle the judgment.

If you own a car, you may not want to surrender the car voluntarily. Usually, if the car is worth less than one thousand dollars, no attempt will be made to seize the car. It would cost about $500 to have someone repossess ("repo") your car. They must take possession of the vehicle and process the paperwork that enables the sheriff to sell the vehicle at auction. If your car is worth $1,000, the net proceeds might be about $500. If you owe more than $500 on the collection account, it might not be feasible to have the car repo'd and sold. If you owe less than $500, it might work for the collection agency. If you own an expensive car and have clear title, you could lose your car through such a proceeding. If you own an expensive car and still owe a big balance against it, your car might not be a repo risk. The collection agencies will be right on top of this, trying to get some payment for their pocket and their client's.

The bill collector and sheriff can seize other items of value, in order to satisfy a judgment. These items might be: jewelry, televisions, stereos, computers, certain clothing and household furniture. These items must have reasonable value. Many items together will help make a reasonable dollar amount for the sheriff to attach. A person could lose many items through a judgment sale.

WARNING! If you suspect that a satisfaction of judgment is pending against you, get rid of your valuable property! You should not have much property of value for someone to attach through judgment. If you have been out of work for some time, you probably do not have much left anyhow.

If some creditors are ready to seek satisfaction of judgment, maybe it is time for you to consider filing BK. Remember, as soon as you file BK, these legal and collection matters are put on hold, or stopped completely.

9
How To Get Lost

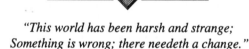

"This world has been harsh and strange;
Something is wrong; there needeth a change."
— Robert Browning

Some people do not handle stress very well. Continual financial stress can lead to Chronic Fatigue Syndrome and other serious illnesses. The only way that some people can deal with their situation is to get away from it. A short or long term respite from credit problems might help some people. So some people decide to "get lost." Many people walk away from their present life and start over elsewhere.

If you do decide to get lost, you need to realize that people will try to find you. There are many ways the credit system and law enforcement can find you. However, if you are very careful, it might take them many years to find you. If you are lucky, they might never find you.

If you want some privacy and enough time to consider your situation, this book will provide ideas to help you. If you want to get lost, you will find tips on what others have done to get lost. If you want to hide, you must think about several important factors. You must consider how you will approach each of the following subject areas.

Post Office Box

Before moving to a new location, you must establish a Post Office Box in an area near your intended destination. You will have to provide your current address as your verifiable street address. This single act is essential. Through this P.O. Box, you will receive letters you want to receive and refuse or throw away mail you do not want.

Getting the P.O. Box might take some time, as there are waiting lists in many cities. In 1994, the fee for a small P.O. Box ranged from about $8 to $35 per year. The fee depends on the city and how the postal service delivers the mail there. Some cities have limited or no rural mail delivery. In those cities, nearly everyone uses a P.O. Box. The box rent is lower for such a city. In a city with full mail delivery service, the box rent will be higher. Once you have your post office location selected, you are then free to move to another home or apartment.

Alternatively, a "mail drop" might be of use to you. Mail drops will cost much more than the average post office box. Mail drops often provide a variety of services for those willing to pay. Later in this chapter, there will be more information about mail drops.

The Rental

You know how much you can afford to pay for rent. You might have to use a sleeping room in someone's home. You might rent a room in a motel or hotel at a monthly rate. You could find an apartment or home. If you are receiving public assistance, you might have to find a way to cover yourself so that your benefits will continue. Failure to disclose your current address or whereabouts to the social service agency could be against the law.

It is possible that credit snoops and others trying to find you might be able to get your address from someone they know at the social service agency. Most social service agencies have reasonable security and secrecy. However, it might not be possible to withhold your residence information from police agencies. For example, a credit snoop might have a friend working as a police officer. That person might get your address through the social service agency.

Most social service agencies prefer to deal with a street address. You need them to send everything to a P.O. Box. How do you get them to do that? Tell them you are concerned about the safety of the mail. Explain that in your area, some neighbors complain about missing mail. Tell them there is evidence someone vandalized your mail box in the past.

If they refuse to send mail to a P.O. Box, tell them you will pick up the mail at their office. If they do send mail to a P.O. Box, you can consider another move to a less expensive rental arrangement. It will be your choice whether or not you inform them of your new address. Again, not telling them about your move might be against the law. I do not recommend you avoid the law. I am reporting what some people do.

In considering the rental, a good suggestion is to find an area within your rent capability. Also, you should pick an area of high transition. In an area with many people moving in and out all the time, neighbors usually stay to themselves. Of course, there are always exceptions. In any given neighborhood, there will always be one or two people who know everything. No matter what time of day or night, they know who is doing what.

These people usually have a lot of time on their hands and they spend much of it looking out their windows. They may spend their time puttering about in their yard or walking up and down the street. These people are easy to spot if you look for them. You will want to avoid contact with these people. If you do have any contact with them, make it brief. You can be courteous, yet not say much of anything. Do not give these people any information about you that might help others who are looking for you.

You should exercise caution when dealing with landlords. Many landlords are nice and considerate. However, some landlords tend toward being greedy S.O.B.s. There is one common thread that ties all landlords together. Be they young or old, male or female, most landlords appreciate *cash*. Therefore, when you talk to a prospective landlord or agent about the property you are considering, remember cash. Often you can get the monthly rent reduced by offering to pay a few months in advance, in cash.

Sometimes you can negotiate a lower rent if you promise to pay in cash each month. A word of caution is necessary at this point. You must be certain that you are dealing with the landlord or the appointed agent. There are many scams involving rental deposits made to the "landlord."

However, say the rent is $550 per month. Three month's rent totals $1,650. Why not offer the landlord $1,350 cash, on-the-spot, to cover the first three months? Negotiate. You have to try. The object here is to get enough money together to get out of your present problem. Go for the discount on the rent. The landlord may surprise you! Quite often, the sight of cash makes people less firm during negotiations. Most landlords will negotiate a price reduction when you wave cash in front of their face. Remind the landlord that cash is not traceable and it will not bounce.

The landlord may balk at the suggestion of a cash discount. If this happens, simply put the money back into your pocket and leave. Let the landlord know that you have other rentals to inspect. Then say you might be back. Take a few steps as you prepare to leave. It might not take too many steps before the landlord will speak up and want to arrange something. Once you have established a firm bargaining position, you can usually succeed in negotiating utilities, etc.

The landlord may want credit information. You can supply the names and phone numbers of trustworthy friends. These people can be present or past employers or landlords. If some questions come up about employment, explain that you are not working at the moment. Tell the landlord that you have recently arrived in the area and you are looking for work. Some landlords do not want to rent to someone who is not working. Explain that your reason for moving to that particular town is the availability of jobs in your field.

Tell the landlord that you are paying the rent in advance, so that you will have the time to find a job without worrying about paying the rent every month. Some landlords require a credit check. **If you allow a credit check, you will tip off every credit snoop about your possible whereabouts.** If the landlord wants a credit check, you will want to pass on that rental.

Some landlords will admire your methodical, careful planning. Others may be suspicious about renting to an unemployed person. If you are working, there should not be a problem. Otherwise, you will have to test the wind in each situation. Landlords in a high transition area are less likely to require detailed information.

This is also true where rooms rent by the week or month. Landlords who rent by the week or month know what to expect! In all cases, it will not hurt to mention any skills you might have in doing home repairs or work in the yard. The handier you are, or say you are, the less reluctant a landlord may be to allow you to rent a place.

In some cases, people will use an assumed name or identity to rent a place to live. This could be against the law in certain areas. You should investigate such matters as they apply to you. You need to know about that before you start a particular course of action. How people establish a fake identity will be discussed later.

The Water Company
And Garbage Company

You should find a rental where the landlord pays the water and garbage. If you start water service in a new area, you may have to give some credit references. Also, you may have to provide background information about yourself. This could include information about employment, previous addresses, etc. You may have to make a deposit to start water, garbage, phone or utilities. Requirements will vary from state to state, and community to community within a state. Sometimes, "Community A" will have a contract with the ABC water company. Two miles away, "Community B" will have service through XYZ water company. Each company may have its own, different requirements for initiating service. Most water companies and other utilities follow regulations set by a state utility commission. Any requirements of the utility usually come from that particular commission or agency.

A word of caution is necessary at this point. If you give any information about yourself to a utility, you could have problems. There is a better than even chance the utility will share this information with the local credit bureau. The local credit bureau will be happy to share the new information with others who might be trying to locate you. Caution and common sense are necessary when dealing with utilities.

To avoid giving out this information, or having to lie about it, find a rental where the utilities are part of the deal. Maybe the landlord will pay for them as long as you pay for the utilities when you pay the rent, like the Smiths did. If the utility bills are in someone else's name, and paid in a timely manner, there should not be a problem.

In some cases, the utility companies may require the tenant's name from the landlord. If you are up front with the landlord, a "Mr. Jones" or "Mrs. Smith" may suffice. You could use your surname only. It is not very likely that utilities will require very much tenant information from the landlord.

If it is not possible to have the utilities paid by the landlord, simply have a trusted friend sign up for the services. When a friend signs for service, all statements will come addressed to that person. You should simply inform the mail carrier that mail in the name of your friend should be forwarded to your P.O. Box. Then tell the post office about your friend "sharing" the box. When you receive a utility bill, go in person and pay cash. Be sure to get a receipt. In many towns and cities, you can pay utility bills at certain banks, drug stores and other retail stores.

Usually, conversation is not necessary, other than pleasantries such as, "Good Morning, I'm paying cash and need a receipt, thank you." All you do is hand over the bill and the money, get your receipt and leave. If someone asks you about the matter, you can always say you are a friend. It is common to have a friend or relative pay the bill for the person named on the statement.

The Gas And Electric Companies

These firms are similar to the water and garbage companies. The exception is that deposits are usually much higher. Also, there may be more questions about your background. Again, you should try to get the gas and electric accounts in the name of the landlord or a trusted friend.

If you paid for the first month, last month and deposit in cash, it is very likely the landlord will honor your request. You must convince the landlord that you will have a money order prepared for the utility payments if the landlord contacts you before collecting the rent. You could provide the landlord with a stamped, self-addressed envelope, prepared for mailing the utility payment. The landlord can do that and know the payment is on its way to the utility. If the landlord does not want to honor your request, you will have to use the help of a friend.

The Phone Company

In most areas, the phone company is real tough. They require a deposit of as much as $200, sometimes more, depending on the applicant's credit history. In addition to the deposit, most phone companies will require significant background information about their prospective customer. It is not likely that you can convince your landlord to subscribe to phone service on your behalf. Therefore, you will need the help of your trusted friend.

Preferably, this friend will have good, established credit references, *and no phone company problems.* Have this friend order the phone with an unlisted phone number. A question could come up about why your friend needs a phone in ABC city. After all, your friend lives in XYZ city. The friend can say the new address is for a writing or painting studio, where peace and quiet are desirable. The phone company should not ask too many questions after getting your friend's explanation.

Usually, all the normal charges associated with connecting service to a residence will apply. You should give your friend cash, so the friend can make an offer to pay the phone company installation charges in advance. You could go with your friend and be a party to the conversation. If something unusual comes up, you could always say to your friend, "Well, if it were up to me, I would..." In that way, there would be fewer mistakes regarding the type of service desired, etc.

Remember, when ordering the phone, specify a private line and an unlisted phone number. Most phone companies charge extra for these services. Some phone companies refer to unlisted phone numbers as non-published phone numbers. Your phone company should provide a standard directory to the service area. Your unlisted, or non-published, phone number will not be in that directory.

However, there are other directories. There are many companies collecting information for their private directories. Some of these look like regular phone books. Others are a cross reference book. Those books cross file information by phone number and street address. Other directories concentrate on a particular geographical area, with listings like the "regular phone book." DO NOT volunteer any information to any of the directory services!

Remember, once you move to a new location, do not give any information to anyone, regardless of who they say they are or what they say they are doing. You should be polite about it, so as not to arouse suspicion of any kind. You should avoid any contact with door to door sales people, pollsters, religious organizations, etc. Certain religious groups keep very accurate records. They know who lives where, and what their recruitment prospects are.

Never give your Social Security number to claim a prize. In fact, the prize may sound too good to be true. If the prize sounds very good, it probably is not true. Even law enforcement knows that people are gullible. Law enforcement is successful at catching many criminals through contest scams. Mail delivered to the wanted person describes some fabulous prize the person has won — vacation trip, new car, etc. When the person shows up to claim the prize, the cops are waiting, arms outstretched! You would think that, after seeing this on TV several times, criminals would be a little more cautious! This is a message to you, so you will be cautious if someone contacts you by phone or mail.

There are many ways for people to trace a phone number to an address, and vice versa. The phone company has this information, and can release the information to "appropriate authorities." There are lists of phone company phone numbers that nearly anyone can call. People can say they are a police officer and get the information they want.

However, this is getting more difficult to do. Now, phone companies have advanced computerized telecommunications equipment. Usually, when someone calls the phone company asking for such information, the operator can tell what phone number that person is using. If you say you are a cop, you should be calling from the police station.

With your phone number in the name of another person, it will be very difficult for someone to find you through that phone number. *WARNING! If you give your phone number to family or friends, a good snoop might be able to track you.* A credit snoop will get the information from the phone bills of your family and friends.

Some people plan on not having a phone. That can present a problem during job searching. You could get by with a message number. If you have to make long distance phone calls to contact family and friends, it is a good idea to use a pay phone. You must use a phone in a different area for each call. There will be more about phones later.

If you move into a residence, with all the utilities in the names of others, no one will know where you are. Exceptions are the landlord and your trustworthy friend(s) or family. It will be possible to elude anyone for a considerable length of time, as in the Smith example. Remember, most utility companies require their workers to wear a photo ID. If someone visits from a utility company, take the time to make a good inspection of their ID. Make sure that it is genuine and fits with the person's drivers license and uniform. It is easy for someone to get fake ID. The meter reader could be someone looking for you. More about fake ID later.

Moving Companies

You should be careful if you plan to use the services of a moving company, or a recognizable truck rental firm. Everyone in your present neighborhood will see that you are moving. Neighbors like to talk about other neighbors. There are hundreds of ways for someone to use a ruse to ask the neighbors questions about you. Although your neighbors may not know where you moved, they might remember that it was 12345 moving company or truck rental firm.

Such an innocent observation on the part of one neighbor may lead the credit snoops to your new front door. Here are some typical ruses used by process servers and credit snoops. They may claim your rented truck or moving van hit their car. They will say they parked their car on the street where you used to live. Also, they may say they have a deposit they need to return to you. Although some may do it, few credit snoops pass themselves off as law enforcement officers. Credit snoops can be real nasty and threaten legal action against someone if they do not provide certain information. You must be very careful with any information you give to anyone. Stick very closely to the "need to know" principle.

An important consideration in moving is to have nothing or very little to move. Many people who may want to get lost will consider selling almost everything they have. Thus, if you still owe money on a bed or television, you should pay for those items before selling them. Or you could call the company where you bought the items, tell them you cannot make the payments, and ask them to come to get their merchandise. (They call this a voluntary repossession.)

If your purchase was through a VISA or MASTERCARD, you could have a problem doing this. In that case, it would be better to pay off the items, then sell them. If your purchase was through a retail store card, or a local account, you could ask them to pick up the merchandise. Usually, the retailer where you purchased the item will be glad to pick up their merchandise. In other cases, they may not bother with it. At that point, you could leave the item behind or take it with you. You should give the entire range of options serious consideration.

When people think of *"bare essentials,"* many items will come to mind. Take with you only the items you really need and upon which you depend. Sell, give to charity, or throw away the rest of your belongings. In almost any community, there is at least one church organization that has a thrift shop. Such a place will be most happy to take items you no longer need. Flea markets and garage or yard sales are a good way of getting rid of everything. Additionally, you will raise some much-needed cash. *WARNING! DO NOT HOLD A "MOVING SALE."* A moving sale could tip people off that you are actually planning to move.

The items that do not move at your sales can be given away or discarded. Remember that church thrift shops and garage sales can be a source of items. You may need furniture and such, after your move. It is OK to have your new residence furnished in "early garage sale."

Such recycling of durable goods aids the economy. Those sales provide extra cash to those who would not otherwise have that cash.

The Post Office

The postal system does not have a very accurate record keeping system. The post office is like a computer: garbage in, garbage out. When you prepared to leave your present address, you rented a P.O. Box in an area near your intended new residency. Unless you inform the post office of your new location, they will still have your old street address on their records. People should inform the post office of changes in address. On the other hand, many people are "forgetful" and might not get around to changing their address for weeks, months, maybe never.

Your post office box "rent due" notice always shows up in your P.O. Box. Seldom are there any questions about your present address when you pay the box rent. I know of some people who have several post office boxes scattered around the various western states. One friend has six P.O. Boxes that have a residence address in Portland, Oregon. This person has not lived there for more than ten years! This person uses these post office boxes for various business interests. P.O. Boxes spread out over certain locations could assist you in the construction of a fake job history.

Once your P.O. Box is in use, you can use it for a "mail address," or a "permanent address." Forms you fill out, such as work applications, insurance, drivers license update, etc., could have the post office address. It is very common for a person new to an area to have no phone number. Those folks could have a *temporary address* where they will be staying for a few days. In those instances, people seldom question the P.O. Box address. Some people believe the less you tell the post office, the more you will perpetuate their inefficiency.

By now, the post office system does not know of your actual whereabouts, other than your former street address and your current P.O. Box. Some people, especially law enforcement officials, and in some cases, process servers can succeed in getting information about you through the post office. The typical credit snoop ruse is to go to the post office and say they ordered products through your P.O. Box.

Then they say the items never arrived. At that point, the snoop asks whether or not there is a possibility of fraud. Some postal investigators are very secretive, others are quite talkative. The latter usually spill all they know, trying to prove they are doing a good job for the person reporting the incident. Also, such snooping can and does extend to private mail drops. If the question of postal fraud comes up, the post office has the right to get the current information on file with the private mail drop service. Also, the post office will disclose any information concerning the box holder to the person making the complaint.

Here is something else you can do to throw off the credit snoops. Put in a change of address to a friend's post office box in another city at least sixty miles away. Someone could really throw off the investigators by putting in a change of address in care of "general delivery," to some obscure town in another state. However, such an act could be against the law. You should investigate the matter before deciding a course of action.

Receiving mail in your name in care of "general delivery" would make an interesting day for the postal employee at Wolf Creek, Montana, or Magnolia, Arkansas, or Rhododendron, Oregon, and other places. Did you know that mail in general delivery has to sit for awhile before the postal system can return it? If you send in another change of address to a city near the one you selected the last time, the snoop might get the idea that you are in the new area, and that you are moving from place to place.

Mail Drops And Mail Forwarding

In most cities of 25,000 or more, there is at least one mail drop company or mail forwarding service. If not, there must be a mail drop in the nearest larger city. Once again, you provide your soon-to-be-vacated street address as your verifiable address. When you move, the mail drop company has the old information.

For many years, people used mail drops and mail forwarding services for privacy, or convenience, or both. Most of these companies operate at a respectable sounding street address. For example, a mail drop might have an address of 500 Smith Street. Your address within that address can be whatever you need that sounds good. Your postal box at the mailing service or mail drop could be the number 12. With such a number, you could use: Suite Twelve, Suite 12, etc. Also, you could use the street address of 500 Smith Street. The mail drop manager will know who you are and which box belongs to you.

These mail drop firms must maintain meticulous records. If you have your mail sent to a mail drop or a mail forwarding service, it will be a good idea to let them know about your "authentic" P.O. Box. Usually, these firms provide other services in addition to mail drop or forwarding. For an extra monthly charge, you can phone and ask if there is mail for you. Some firms allow you to call and have your mail read to you. Also, you can stop by and check the mail box regularly. It is a good idea to visit occasionally and get the mail yourself.

Someone might visit the mail drop or mail forwarding service, inquiring about your whereabouts. The credit snoop will not get very far with the average mail drop manager. However, the same snoop could go to the postal inspectors with a rigged up story about the possibility of fraud. If the postal inspector investigates possible "fraud through the mail," the mail drop manager will have to disclose your information file.

At that point, all anyone would have is your old street address and the old phone number. Your present "authentic" P.O. Box would show the same information. Your address information would be a dead lead for anyone looking for you. The postal authorities and the mail drop manager had dated information about you. Now you would be in a firm position to receive mail selectively. You could keep the mail you wanted and discard or return all mail that looked suspicious.

A word of caution is necessary here. Professional snoops can be very creative in trying to discover your whereabouts. You could receive a very large envelope. You could receive an odd-sized package, maybe a mailing tube. The piece of mail could be bright, colored, almost festive in appearance. If you leave the post office or mail drop service carrying such an item, you run the risk of someone identifying you.

Ordinarily, the credit snoop would not know what you look like. The message here is to examine your mail with no one else around you. Always take a large shopping bag with you and place your mail in it. That will hide your mail as you leave the building. Never walk out into the open carrying anything that could identify you to a credit snoop.

Drivers License And Auto Registration

When you move, you should report your change of address to the department of motor vehicles or drivers license bureau. Most states have requirements to do this within a certain number of days. When you get your P.O. Box, you should notify the appropriate agencies of your "change of address." Go ahead and send in notification of your new mailing address. This will provide correct information for your drivers license and auto registration. Any information sent by these departments will reach you quickly, at your P.O. Box.

Most address change requirements refer to your street address. However, what if you are traveling? What if you are staying with friends for a short time? What if you are homeless, except for your vehicle? There are many reasons for not listing a street address. Some people give the address of a motel, where they might stay for a short time. They provide the motel with a forwarding address (the P.O. Box) in case any mail comes to the motel. Other people give the address of a friend. Again, I am not recommending that you do this. I am only reporting what some people do.

Many private investigators and credit snoops have immediate access to license and automobile registration information. Almost anyone can obtain the information on a drivers license or vehicle license by sending a required fee to the appropriate state agency. Anyone doing this will receive your old street address and your new "mailing address." Of course, many people are quite forgetful. It could take weeks, months, even years, before you remember to send in a change of address for your drivers license. In this case, your promptness in reporting the new "mailing address" will serve two purposes. You provided proper notice to authorities, and you provided a dead lead to all others.

In most states, you will be partially in compliance with the law by writing your new mailing address on the drivers license and vehicle registration. What if a police officer asks you about the address during a traffic stop? You reply that you have recently moved, and that the move is only temporary while you are looking for a permanent place to live.

If you do not send in a change of address, especially during automobile registration renewal time, such action could be against the law. However, I am sure the average police officer has heard the full range of excuses. The police hear about the person forgetting to put the change of address on the license, or forgetting to send in the change of address. The main point to remember is to make it look accidental or unintentional.

In some states or counties, providing proof of an insurance policy may be a requirement. This may happen at the time of registration renewal. Also, such information may always have to be in the vehicle. This information could help someone doing a cross reference check of names and addresses. In most situations where a person has a car or truck, insurance is a must. When you buy the insurance, you must be careful not to let the agent get too much information from you. This information will find its way into computer files.

Once there, the information will be available to anyone. Investigators and credit snoops will take advantage of every opportunity to get information about you. It is possible to purchase insurance for your car or truck without letting others know about your present situation. Again, people use the old "street address" and the new P.O. Box. You must tell the insurance people about your "mailing address."

Licensing Bureaus

For employed and self-employed people, it may be necessary to list information about yourself. Your address and phone number may be a requirement by a city, county or state agency. Remember, this information becomes public information and anyone can gain access to it. If you have a license to operate a small business, this information is public information. Usually, you will be able to get by with the old street address and your new P.O. Box.

Another way of dealing with licensing involves lack of information and/or misinformation. People who do not want certain types of information known to a licensing bureau or agency find a way to circumvent the requirement. They use their old street address, a motel address, or the address of a friend. If the information will be going by mail, some people leave certain questions unanswered. Depending on the laws in your area, such a simple act could be illegal. Again, many people are forgetful. It could take a long time to inform an agency about a change of address.

If you have any contact with a licensing situation, such as business, auto, or drivers licensing or registration, find a way to code your name. If you keep a file of such activity, you can learn who released your name to other agencies or businesses. This could be very helpful in determining who is giving information to the credit snoops and others trying to find you.

Every state in the United States has a Department of Motor Vehicles, or something similar. The DMV serves as a clearing house of information for law enforcement agencies. Also, the DMV may have miscellaneous regulatory responsibilities. It is possible to get a person's address from the DMV. In most states, the DMV will require the payment of a fee for this service.

When you need this type of information, you simply write a letter saying someone left a note on your windshield. Someone mentioned that a vehicle, license number @#$%!&*, damaged your vehicle. You need the name and address of the registered owner. Under these circumstances, you will probably get that information.

An Attorney

An attorney may be able to help you in several ways. First, an attorney can counsel you regarding your rights within the credit system. Second, an attorney can advise you about the appropriateness of bankruptcy. (Remember, in the Smith example, two different attorneys advised them to use bankruptcy protection, many months before they filed BK.)

However, Mr. Smith held the pig-headed idea that he could handle everything himself. Somehow, he was sure he could pay all of his debts. This attitude cost the Smiths their house and most of their personal property of any value. There was no money to pay bills in a timely manner. There were times the Smiths had to sell a table, the couch, or a dresser so they could pay the rent or buy food. Those people who are working, but cannot manage their debts, should see an attorney. It is better to get some quick advice about reasonable alternatives.

If you own real property or are buying a home, an attorney could help you. An attorney can put the property up for sale on your behalf. Also, the attorney could help you rent the property. An attorney can help you with advice about "homesteading" your property. An attorney can help you include the property in the bankruptcy.

An attorney can act as your agent and sell your real or personal property for you. You can sign a document called "power of attorney." This is a declaration authorizing someone else to act on your behalf. They can do that for a specific transaction or event. You give your attorney, or another person, complete charge or control over the sale. People trying to find you will have to deal with the attorney. Normally, your attorney is not under any obligation to disclose your whereabouts.

When the transaction is done, the attorney will deduct his or her fee and send you a check for the net proceeds. Most attorneys will not charge you a fee for a few minutes of consultation. However, most attorneys will charge at least $25 for a visit of fifteen to thirty minutes. This amount will vary with different attorneys.

There is a client "agency" created by working with an attorney. Credit snoops, even law enforcement officials, might have trouble getting information about you from your attorney. For an appropriate fee, an attorney might act as your mail forwarding address. For example, Bob Smith, c/o John Jones, Attorney at Law, 500 Jones Street.

This could have a dual benefit. First, you have another address to throw off the credit snoops. Second, anyone trying to find you, particularly a credit snoop, might suffer the *AW SHIT*! syndrome. If they see you are having "all your mail" sent to an attorney, they might think you are planning to file BK. Many attorneys will have their BK clients' mail forwarded to the attorney's office. That act in itself could cause some credit snoops and collectors to give up the chase.

An attorney can serve as an effective screen on your behalf. You can be thousands of miles away and have your affairs handled properly. You can mantain regular contact with your attorney. You can be informed about important matters, like court dates. Also, you will stay current with the attorney's efforts to sell real or personal property for you. This is important if selling such property is part of your plan to get lost.

The "normal" attorney, if there is such a person, may not want to take your case. You should shop around and try to find an attorney who is willing to help you. You should provide full disclosure of your plans to the attorney. A good bet is to check with the attorneys who specialize in BK. They are familiar with credit problems, and the tactics used by the credit community. Such an attorney may be more understanding about why someone would want to get lost.

To summarize this chapter, you now have an understanding of the basics of getting lost. You know how some people establish a new mailing address through a P.O. Box. You know how some people find a place to live. You know how some people get a *really* unlisted phone number, by having it in another person's name. You know what some people look out for when moving day comes. You know what some people give and do not give to the post office. You know how some people use mail drops and mail forwarding services. You know how some people deal with their drivers license and vehicle registrations. You know how some people deal with licensing bureaus. You know how some people will try to get the help of an attorney.

The steps to getting lost are simple. You need to give very careful thought to the matter. Anyone can get lost. The methods I described so far are *lightweight.* That is because the methods described are not permanent, merely temporary.

If someone wants to get lost for a long time, they must change their ID. They will have to become a "new person," just like the government secret witness relocation program participants. The person wanting to "get lost" will have to develop a new identity, job history, and relocate to another area.

Again, the author and publisher do not recommend that people break any laws. This book only reports what others have done. For example, in the last year or two, several people came forward out of hiding. In one case, a woman was on the F.B.I.'s wanted list for many years. She "became another person," in a state far from her former life. Furthermore, she was a model citizen in her new life. In another case, a man "became another person," in a state far from his former life. He hid from law enforcement for about 18 years! During that time he assumed at least two identities. Again, this person led a model existence.

Did you know you could be living next door to a convicted murderer? Yes, one of your close neighbors could be a former mobster. He may have beaten, raped and killed in his past life. Due to testifying against his former associates, he now has a "new life."

Yes, our government provides a new identity for such people. They get a new name, new Social Security number, new job history, etc. The government even provides a "stipend," or allowance, while the former mobster or racketeer "adjusts to a new lifestyle."

On the other hand, an ordinary person, troubled by debt, wanting to establish a "new life," could get into trouble with the government. How does that make you feel? It does look like there might be some inconsistency in what is fair and reasonable.

10
How They Can Find You

"Two things only a man cannot hide:
that he is drunk, and that he is in love."
— Antiphanes of Macedonia

The credit bureaus and collection agencies have ample motivation to find you. By using personal investigation techniques, computers and the cooperation of law enforcement agencies (or "friendly access" to law enforcement information), credit bureaus and collection agencies will do their best to find you. Remember that anything associated with credit information and computers can lead the credit snoops to your door. Usually, investigators used by the collection process are very thorough. They may get paid by commission or bonus. Sources of their information, again, would be: your former landlord, former employer, former spouse, relatives, neighbors, etc. An investigator will check every conceivable lead, in case someone may know some tiny bit of information about you.

The positive side is this: if you follow the actions successfully used by others, you should be able to throw these people off your trail. It is especially helpful to set up a series of mail drops and P.O. Boxes in various areas. I would be willing to bet that for every person "found" by a collection agency, there are many open files.

Banks, Credit Card Companies And Personal Finance Companies

These institutions, and some retailers, are often very reluctant to share information about a particular client. Most credit granting companies provide regular reports on all their customers to the credit bureaus. If John Doe phones and wants to know something about Mary Smith, chances are that he will not learn much. However, many of the people who work in credit departments earn low wages for doing a very depressing job. Someone might come along with an offer of $100 or $200 and tempt the right person. The average person might have trouble doing that. However, a private investigator, process server, credit bureau or collection agency might be successful in getting any information they want.

At banks and other financial institutions, you can have checks printed with just your name, without your address. You can list your P.O. Box as the mailing address for statements and other bank business. Also, some banks will hold your statements, so you can pick them up in person. When you anticipate your move, you should notify the bank, credit card companies, and other financial institutions of your new "mailing address," and give them your P.O. Box. In this way, you will receive correspondence from those companies and not miss anything of importance.

The banks have investigators and very well-staffed credit departments. Again, they will use any method available to try to locate your whereabouts. Someone checking your references in various ways could end up at a former bank. That bank could be looking for you, and a simple credit reference could lead the credit snoops to you. It is very possible that paperwork involved with financial institutions has a time value attached to it. If someone cannot find you within six months to a year, your file will probably lose its importance. Your file will remain open for some time. However, the energy spent on your file will decrease over time. They will spend more time dunning and going after accounts when the bank knows how to find the person.

In recent years, banks have started accepting more information from companies outside of banking. They subscribe to information services in an attempt to have the most current information available.

For example, some banks and mortgage banks make "government" real estate loans. Those are the FHA and VA type of guaranteed loan programs. (That means the FHA or VA will guarantee a certain portion of the loan amount. This is done to minimize the bank's potential loss in case of foreclosure.) With a name and Social Security number, the lender will instantly know if the borrower has defaulted on a student loan or past mortgage obligation. With the improvements in communications and computers, what used to take days or weeks now takes seconds.

Friends, Family, Neighbors, Business Acquaintances

There's an old saying, "In time of prosperity friends will be plenty; In time of adversity not one in twenty," attributed to James Howell. That statement has a certain ring of truth to it. Especially when you reflect on the friends or relatives you *believe* you can count on for some help when the going gets tough. Therefore, it might not surprise you if you experience some disappointments along the way. Even your parents and brothers or sisters might turn away from you when you ask them for help.

When you anticipate your move, carefully select certain friends and relatives and let them know your new "mailing address." Simply explain that you plan to relocate soon, but you have not found a place to live yet. However, anyone can reach you through the P.O. Box. Ingrained in nearly everyone's mind are the words, "keep in touch," as advertised by the telephone companies.

Modern day dependency on the telephone is nearly a conditioned response, not unlike Pavlov's dogs. Similarly, there is a "need" to mail letters if a person cannot contact you by phone. Take the time to let everyone know how they can keep in touch with you. Thus, you will have created the appearance of not trying to "get lost." Furthermore, you will avoid the suspicion attached to people who do not have a telephone. Nowadays, very few people can get by without a telephone. Most people do not understand why someone would not have a telephone in their home.

A simple rule here is: do not give your phone number to *anyone*. That means not one person. In some cases, that one person you think you can trust will disappoint you. People within your own family can inadvertently betray your new location. If you have any suspicion that a family member might not be reliable with your new information, do not let that person know anything about you. You can bet that credit snoops will try to contact your family members, in their attempts to locate you.

The reasons for contacting you can seem real. Credit snoops will have authentic looking ID, and a plausible excuse or *need* to locate you. These ruses of needing to get in touch with you can vary. They may include your work, hobbies, general lifestyle, past (an old friend from school or the military). Also, the credit snoop may use your past community work, volunteer work, affiliation with churches, service clubs, even your practice of donating blood. A good credit snoop will try every trick in the book to try to locate your whereabouts. Remember, there is money in it for the credit snoop.

Through careful checking of credit applications and other documents in which you listed a friend or relative as a reference, the credit snoops will have people to contact. Of course, your former neighbors and employers may also be sources. Any of those people might accept the $50 to $100 offered by the credit snoop, to provide the lead needed to find you.

Can you imagine a good friend of yours being contacted by an "investigator" for a major hospital? There is an urgent need to contact you regarding a blood donation you made several weeks ago! Something about HIV, and it is an emergency, and he or a member of his staff must contact you. Would your friend spill the beans or say nothing and then let you know what happened?

Would your friend know there could be an illegal tap on his phone, and that by calling you he would lead the snoop to your new address? Would your friend know the credit snoop might be sitting in a car across the street? The investigator could have a listening device capable of hearing conversations inside your friend's house. This type of intrusion happens in the movies, and in real life as well. If you can imagine the circumstances the chances are a credit snoop could use it.

If you contact someone by phone and they want your phone number, simply say that you are calling from the home of a friend. Tell them you cannot give out that phone number. You could say you are calling from a pay phone, because you do not have a phone yet. A good trick is to tape record about ten minutes of "background noise." You can use normal street traffic at a busy intersection, or the noise in a restaurant or cocktail lounge. You can play that noise during your phone conversations. This will make it sound as if you are actually calling from a pay phone near an airport, bus terminal, bar, restaurant, or busy street. This also can help keep your phone calls brief.

Again, your former neighbors and employers, relatives, and close family members are often very glad to talk about you. Credit snoops can pose in many disguises, with properly "rigged-up" business cards and ID. The credit snoop will start gathering information from those sources first. If the only information anyone knows is your P.O. Box mailing address, you have an excellent chance of staying hidden.

Your Enemies

Sometimes humans harbor thoughts of vengeance. Particularly people who have some sort of grudge against another person. There are some people walking around who have no enemies. However, few people can say they do not have at least one enemy. A trusted friend could be an enemy and you may not know it. All of your known and unknown enemies may be very glad to say something about you, as a way of revenge.

This could come from something real or imagined that you may have done to them. You could your friends and enemies alike that you are moving to Carson City, Nevada. Tell them you have a job waiting for you at a gambling resort. That would throw everyone off the track.

Offered the opportunity, your enemies may take delight in embellishing stories they know or have heard about you. Credit information collectors and insurance investigators have a notorious reputation for going after juicy gossip. Remember, rumors, half-truths, or outright lies can become near fact when included in credit and investigative reports.

Grocery And Other Retail Stores

Grocery stores, the local liquor store, deli, bar and other places where you shop regularly may look very harmless. Many of the owners, managers or employees of those establishments may know more about you than you think. If those people see you frequently, you may occasionally talk with them. These places of business can be a large encyclopedia of information about you and your personal habits! Someone tracing your movements and personal activities may try for information from these sources. A careless comment to a clerk or store manager about your upcoming move to XYZ City could be trouble. You may have known the person for a long time and consider them a friend. Your careless comment might be remembered by one of these people. Also, you could have information on file with these stores. There may be some information about check cashing, local charge accounts or special orders.

Often, these people know the type of car you drive. They also might know your favorite brands of cigarettes, liquor, soft drinks, clothes, cameras, etc. These are pieces of information that can follow you to your new location. The suggestion here is to make a list of all items you routinely use. You should plan to make some changes.

If you smoke a particular brand of cigarette, change to another brand. Better yet, stop smoking. A credit snoop could learn that you like to drink Green's Miracle Tonic and smoke Smoggem cigarettes. If you carry those habits to your new location, you could be assisting someone trying to find you. If the credit snoop is sure you are within a certain area, it is easy to ask various retail outlets if they are selling any Green's Miracle Tonic or Smoggem cigarettes. The credit snoop may find a store that has started selling more of those brands. Also, the credit snoop may learn that a store has a regular customer for those brands. If so, the investigator will try to get additional information.

It is better to maintain a polite relationship with the people in stores. Do not let them know you will be moving. On the other hand, you could tell them you will be moving to a town five hundred miles away in the opposite direction of your true destination. Better yet, tell them you are moving to another state. Anyone approaching these people for information will be thrown off the track.

· Many credit snoops and others looking for you will rely on the information they get from store employees as "good" information. The investigators will believe the information is from a "reliable source." After all, why would the manager of a store lie about your whereabouts? False information "planted" in as many places as possible will send the credit snoops on a wild goose chase!

Medical Records And
Social Security Numbers

If you are in hiding and require medical services, remember that a hospital may require your Social Security Number (SSN). The medical community and insurance companies routinely share information with other insurance companies and credit/collection agencies. In this age of computerized information services, you could have a credit snoop knocking on your door in a day or two.

Nearly all insurance companies require your Social Security Number. They do this primarily for additional policy holder identification. The solution here is obvious. Simply refuse to provide your SSN to anyone. Two exceptions may be your employer and the IRS. However, some people refuse to provide their SSN to their employer or the IRS. Sometimes those people use a made up number or the number of a relative.

Usually, your employer will provide your SSN and employment information to the company's medical insurance carriers. Once this happens, the information could spread to other sources. If that happens, you could eventually see a summons served at your job, or an in-person visit by a credit snoop.

Some people recommend using a made up SSN. They memorize or write the number on a piece of paper. Many people do not carry their Social Security card with them. That is not unusual. Few employers bother to check an applicant's SSN. Few employers actually look at the number for visual verification. These practices may change in the future. Some employers may want to see your SSN before they hire you. Those people who recommend using another number, prefer to use the number of one of their children. Also, they may use the number of a brother, sister, or parent. Sometimes, the number they make up is just a few digits different from their real number. That allows for claiming they made a mistake in giving their SSN to someone, if the discrepancy is ever noticed.

Many people have no faith in the Social Security program. There is a realization the system may go broke before they can receive any benefits. These people rationalize, "What's the difference, anyway?" To them, it does not matter which account number gets the earnings credit, because the system is going broke.

When the federal government comes looking for you, they will do anything to secure an arrest. Every conceivable cause for arrest will be available to them. Some time ago, a woman was the object of a nationwide hunt. She had something to do with an alleged extortion plot. The Feds arrested her for using a false SSN. That was done as part of the arrest procedure to make sure there was a valid arrest. **WARNING. *It is against the law to use a false SSN or one that does not belong to you.*** You must decide what action you want to take, after learning the possible consequences you might experience.

Some people deal with the requirement for a SSN in the following way. They have the SSN memorized and kept in a safe place. If someone asks for their SSN, they tell them the number they memorized. What if someone asks to see their card? The person says they do not have the SSN with them. Then they say the SSN is in a bank safety deposit box for safe keeping. Then they name a location of a bank in a distant city. It would take several days to travel there and get the card.

With hospitals, you will probably have to pay the bills in cash anyhow. If you are on public assistance, then they would already have your SSN, or the number that was provided to the social service agency. That number will be part of your medical stickers.

If you continue using your real SSN, and have skipped out on support payments or a government guaranteed loan, someone may find you very quickly. The district attorney who has jurisdiction over the collection of your support payments has access to government files about you. Also, government bill collectors have access to this information. Your employer must report your SSN as a new hiree within the required quarterly reporting period. Once that happens, it is just a matter of time before the government knows your whereabouts. For that reason, some people change jobs and move about every four or five months.

Remember, your medical records are not as private as you may believe. You could have signed a release form, allowing the release of your medical information. Chances are, everything in your medical file is in a computer database. Most doctors are very careful about releasing information. They usually only release information about a particular injury or illness.

However, some medical staff personnel may not be very careful. Worse yet, a person working for the doctor may send copies of the entire file. Once this information gets into the computer database, seldom does it leave. It is very difficult to get inaccurate information corrected, once the information is in the insurance/medical/credit snoop databases.

Welfare Records

Usually, public assistance records are moderately secure. However, it is possible that someone may accept a cash offer for information. Again, the average person may not be as successful as the professional at getting public assistance records. In most states, there is a sharing of information between Social Security and social service agencies. The curiosity comes primarily from the social service agency. They want to make sure you report all of your income. Also, the social service agency will usually cooperate with the county district attorney. They do this to help track fathers who have skipped and are not paying court ordered child support. You can see how someone may use the computer information network, between agencies, to track a person. Usually, that process requires a SSN.

A finance company manager informed me that finance companies can usually locate a person almost immediately, using social service information or Social Security numbers. He refused to say how this is done, but did appear serious about the remark. When I offered to bet him $25,000 that I could disappear for one year without him finding me, he refused the bet. He claimed that it would be too easy, like taking candy from a baby. However, I do not share his outlook.

Credit & Teller Machine Cards

Credit card companies focus in three areas. In addition to teller machine cards, there are bank cards, retail cards and travel & entertainment cards. These card operations have staffs capable of tracking your movements. If the credit system is looking for you, they can track you if you use your cards. Your use of the cards may tell them where you are going.

The use of the cards can also indicate your present location. Much depends on how quickly your card activity shows up in the record system. It is common for police to know that a possible crime victim used their teller machine card at 8:42 AM, last Tuesday, at ABC bank branch in a certain city. Credit cards can provide such information just about as quickly.

There are some good reasons for keeping at least one credit card, even if you do not use it very often. Many hotels and motels in this country will not let you spend the night with them, unless you have a credit card! Even if you have lots of cash! Even if you are willing to pay an extra deposit! You can present your card in such a situation. Of course, this is under the provision that the room, or car rental, does not exceed the credit limit.

Often the credit card has a dollar limit per transaction, and the business must call for credit approval or clearance if the purchase is over a certain amount. Some establishments require an approval if the charge is more than $25, or $100, etc. Such a phone call could alert credit card security to your present location. It is not uncommon to have the local police hold someone on charges of credit card fraud, due to long distance calls to verify your account!

Nowadays, many businesses have their credit card charges on a computer system. At the point of purchase, your card electronically connects with the card company computer. If there is a problem with your account, the computer does not allow the purchase.

Again, before your departure, notify all of your credit card companies about your new "mailing address." *WARNING! As you go to different areas to check out possible relocation sites, DO NOT USE YOUR CREDIT OR BANK TELLER CARDS.* You do not want any record of where you have been to show up on any of the credit or bank teller card computers.

Some people check their credit card agreements to determine their liability if their card becomes lost or stolen. It may "pay them" to have their credit card "lost or stolen." If you want to get lost, you may want to make a "track." For example, say that a person lives in Chicago, Illinois. That person plans to relocate to a smaller community such as Eureka, California. That person takes a trip to Ft. Lauderdale, Florida, New York City, or New Orleans, Louisiana. That person makes several stops along the way and uses credit cards for small purchases, such as gas and meals. This establishes a "track," to the "destination city."

When the person arrives in the "destination city," they drop their credit cards in a busy place. This may be the bus terminal, the airport, or a downtown sidewalk, etc. That person also could find a real scuzzy neighborhood and drop the cards there.

The chances are almost 100% that someone will pick up those credit cards. They will either turn them in or try to use the cards themselves. They may sell the cards to someone who specializes in using lost or stolen credit cards. Anyone trying to find the person whose name is on the cards will be on a wild goose chase. That person planning to relocate to northern California will have left tracks in New York, Ft. Lauderdale or New Orleans. People wanting to disappear do this all the time.

School Records

If you plan to move as a family unit, you need to arrange to have your children's school records transferred. Usually, this will be done through an inter-district transfer. In some situations, it is possible to request that you personally hand carry the sealed records to the new school. You could say that you are not sure yet exactly where you will live. Let them know that you will be on the road for several weeks, while you look for a job.

State laws and school district regulations may vary, and they may not allow you to hand carry the records. Education laws throughout the states are not consistent. It may be perfectly acceptable to go to a new school district without any records. You could say that you just moved from a state where they would not allow the transfer of the records easily.

If the new school district sends an inquiry out of state, it could take some time before they receive a response. By that time, you may be ready to move on to another location or you could continue the matter. If the district has no record of your children as students, it is easy to say you have no idea how they could have "lost" the records. It could take as long as six to nine months to fix a problem like that.

A persistent credit snoop will call the school districts where you lived, based on your last street address. The investigator will say that he is you, and inquire about why the new school district did not receive the records yet. A good talker may get a school secretary or clerk to disclose where they mailed the records. The person at the school may not be aware of what is happening.

The only way around this is to have a letter from you and your wife on file with the old school and school district. Both of you must sign the letter. The letter should request that under no circumstances should any information about your children go to anyone but you in person. By law, the school and district should not give any information by mail or phone. They should only give information to you when you appear in person, with photo-positive ID. A letter like that should cause a dead end for most investigators. Anyone inquiring by mail would have to have the signatures match. You must not rely entirely on the safety of this method. It is possible that school district employees might be susceptible to money offered for information.

If your children have school and neighborhood friends, it will be necessary for you to maintain secrecy with your children and their friends. A good credit snoop will contact children in the former neighborhood. There is always a chance that one of the kids may know where you moved. Some of the kids may have your new address and phone number. Little playmates like to keep in touch if one moves to another area. Teenagers are particularly insistent on letting their friends know where they have moved. The P.O. Box "mailing address" could be very important in this type of situation.

Although there are laws protecting student privacy in most states, there are ways around these laws. Confidential school records could lead to your exact whereabouts. If any particular part of your plan to get lost goes awry, school records could lead to your discovery. You should research the situation with school records. You need a definite plan about this matter before you decide to relocate to another area.

Another solution to the situation pertaining to children is to have them stay with relatives for some time. This will allow matters to settle down in your new location. Most parents would not want to be away from their children for any length of time. However, having the kids stay with their grandparents or aunt and uncle will provide another false track.

Service Clubs, Alumni Associations And Other Groups

If you are a member of any service clubs or other organizations, you will need to keep a very low profile in your new location. By continuing active membership in a particular group, you could make it possible for someone to track you to your new location. You should make sure that you pay all of your dues, fines and assessments. Then you can resign from the group several weeks later. It may be difficult for you to sever ties with a particular group. You may have spent a lot of time and money with the group.

However, a clean break is a good idea. After you recover from your present financial hardship, or other reasons you may have for getting lost, you can rejoin the organizations. During your recovery period, you should have a clean separation from these groups.

Here is an example of how easy it is for someone to get information about you. Police officers and firefighters usually have unlisted phone numbers. If someone calls the station to get the phone number or address, the caller will not be successful. However, in one example, a person went to a neighboring community and visited the fire station. He said that he was an uncle of a certain firefighter, and was visiting the area. The uncle wanted to see his nephew, but had left the address and phone number at home.

One of the men on duty phoned the other fire department and identified himself. The other fire department provided the non-published phone number of the firefighter in question. The "uncle" was a credit snoop working on a divorce case. He got the phone number without any requirement for identification. That on duty person should have called the other fire department and asked them to have the firefighter call the station where the "uncle" was waiting.

Similarly, almost any firefighter or police officer can get access to phone numbers and street addresses. Someone trying to find you may get your contact information from a police officer or firefighter friend. Again, if you have your phone number in the name of another person, and a P.O. Box address, it will be very hard to find you!

Holidays such as Easter and Christmas are good times for credit snoops and investigators trying to find you. They can always use the ruse that they are a relative wanting to surprise you for Thanksgiving, etc. Usually, people are more tolerant of others requesting information about relatives during the holiday seasons. If you entrusted your contact information to someone, they might be taken off guard during Christmas or another holiday.

Police Records

In your new location, you will have to lead a "model existence" as long as you wish to hide. If you get injured in an auto accident, it may make the news back home. If the police arrest you, it may make the papers in the region. Accidents or arrests involving former residents are likely to make the front page of the small town paper.

Many investigators, bounty hunters and process servers have friends or contacts within the police and fire departments. While it may not be routine, it is very simple for these people to get your name and address from an arrest report or accident report. The city or county communications centers also have information about you. These agencies serve as the dispatchers for public service agencies. They have the authority to contact the phone company for access to non-published phone numbers and address information.

If there is a genuine, verifiable emergency, these communications centers will normally phone the person they need to contact. The communications person will identify himself, explain the nature of the emergency and give the name of the person to contact for further details. Usually, the communications centers will not release information to any third party, except law enforcement personnel. Most any law enforcement agency can get this information immediately — even from state agencies. In such cases, there are ways to verify the authenticity of the out of state agency requiring the information.

If you have a police record, you may have to register at the nearest police department if you relocate. Also, you may have to report to the parole system before moving. You must let them know your intentions, new location, etc. Often, the court may have to approve such a move. Often, as a condition of parole, you might have to report all address and phone number changes. If you try to evade this type of obligation, you could end up in serious trouble. Although many people do skip from this type of obligation, *good advice is: do not do it!* If you get stopped for a minor traffic violation, or eventually caught in some other way, you could end up with automatic confinement. Who needs that?

Most police departments are using advanced computers. It can take a matter of a few seconds to learn all kinds of information about you, particularly if you have any criminal record. A driver's license, SSN, past or present military ID numbers, psychological profiles, arrest records, or fingerprints, all can lead police to your whereabouts. Again, if you have "new information" to cover most of the above sources of police information, it will take a little longer to find you. If your "new information" is good enough, they may never find you!

Your Garbage

Your garbage? Most anyone will recall that certain celebrities and other famous persons get their garbage inspected. Movie stars, major mafia figures and former presidents of the United States have had their garbage sorted and examined by investigative journalists, law enforcement agencies and others.

In fact, one alleged mafia crime boss who lived in Arizona had his garbage picked up by the federal government for about two years. During that time, the FBI and other agencies were able to piece together enough information to get an indictment. Later, the information was enough to convict the mafioso. Former presidents of the United States have had regular trouble with people sorting through the presidential garbage. Someone is always trying to discover juicy gossip about the former president or information about what products they use in their household.

By searching through your garbage, an investigator can learn much about you. If someone sorts through your garbage for many weeks, they will learn about your personal habits. They will learn about what you eat, and your preferences for personal products. They will also learn about where you buy most of your groceries, where you buy gasoline, etc.

Another treasure-trove may routinely found in the garbage is private mail. There could be letters from friends or family, or bills from companies to whom you owe money. Other items may include phone bills, empty prescription containers, banking information, charge card information, etc. If someone finds your phone bill, they can determine where you have been placing calls, how often, and to whom. (They can check the reverse directory for that area, or place a call.) Similarly, relatives who may know of your whereabouts can have their garbage searched. If the relative has phoned you, this information on their phone bill could lead to your discovery.

You can see how important it is to leave no "evidence" behind in the garbage! A simple solution is to have two garbage containers. One will be for wet garbage, for items like unwanted food, cans, bottles, etc. Use the other can for paper products such as receipts from stores, unwanted mail, bills, and any personal refuse such as prescription bottles, etc. If you recycle most of your garbage, you will have neat stacks to help you decide how to dispose of the items.

A metal container with a lid is a good type of container for dry garbage. You must keep the "dry" container in a locked place, such as the back porch or the garage. You must make sure you always use the lid.

You can use a good pair of scissors to cut up paper items such as bills, receipts and mail. Cut those items up as thoroughly as a paper shredder. Once you accumulate a medium-sized pile of paper shreds, burn it in the fireplace or outdoors somewhere. Make sure you are very careful about floating ashes and that they permit outdoor burning in your area. Also, you may know of an area nearby where it would not hurt to discard *small amounts* of paper refuse in proper refuse containers. You may select a handy but remote area to bury the paper garbage.

The point here is to pay attention to your garbage. When you leave your present residence, you must leave everything spotlessly clean. Leave nothing behind that someone can connect to you. If you have any doubts about an item, destroy it or get rid of it through one of the previously discussed methods. If you leave nothing behind, including *clean* garbage cans, there will be nothing that a credit snoop can use to find you.

Sophisticated Surveillance

In some instances, investigators may use special equipment to learn more about you. There are long range listening devices, nicknamed "shotgun mikes," that are available to most anyone, including credit snoops. These devices are similar to a small radar dish and can pick up a conversation for half a mile or more. The hearing distance depends on the quality of the device, any background noise, and atmospheric conditions.

These devices are available through many outlets, including electronics supply stores. In some rare instances, someone may bug your phone lines with an electronic listening device. This is highly illegal without specific warrants or court approval. However, evidence does exist that persons acting outside the law use taps. While these methods may look out of the ordinary for the "average" or "normal" person, some investigators may use equipment like this against you.

Here is one possible situation. A couple has lost their main source of family income. Debts are mounting and going unpaid. Creditors become anxious, and enlist the services of an attorney, an investigator, or a collection agency to try to collect the amount owed. An investigator with modern, technologically advanced, listening equipment could park outside the debtor's home. The investigator could hear conversations while the family eats dinner, or after they go to bed. The listening devices can pry into their private lives. Someone could hear discussions about who to pay and who not to pay. They could hear about any plans to skip town, or where they have any hidden assets, etc. Any conversation that you would ordinarily believe to be private could have another set of ears listening to it, outside the home, listening in.

The message here is this: The small person cannot be too careful. Some people may believe they are immune to such eavesdropping. Undoubtedly, there are millions of people out of work at the present. Credit institutions, process servers, investigators, collectors, bounty hunters, etc., are having to hustle to protect their interests and keep up with the work load.

Remember, these people will resort to almost anything to make a complete or partial collection. They will try any tactic to locate you, if the price is right. You may not be safe within the confines of your own home. It may be better to be on guard about sensitive conversations. Discuss family matters, finances, and other activities, with loud music playing in the background, just as they do in the movies. This may look silly, but it may help protect your privacy.

Be careful about your movements. Most people pay no attention to someone following them. You should always be aware of your surroundings, whether you walk or drive. If you think someone is following or watching you, vary your course or direction several times. If the person continues to follow you, drive to the nearest police station or fire department. Let them know someone is following you. Give them the description of the car and the license plate number. Nowadays, the police are very quick to respond to this type of situation, because carjackings are so common.

To summarize this chapter, you now know some of the tricks used to find someone. Investigators will track you through: credit bureaus, banks, credit card companies, personal finance companies, friends, family, neighbors, business acquaintances, grocery and retail stores, medical records, Social Security numbers, welfare records, school records, service clubs, alumni associations, police records, your garbage, and through sophisticated surveillance. Again, by giving careful thought to the above "possible information contacts" and examining your own situation, you will know what you have to avoid. Also, you will know how, where and when you must provide false leads or "tracks."

11
Establishing Fake Identification

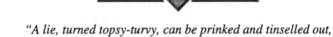

*"A lie, turned topsy-turvy, can be prinked and tinselled out,
decked in plumage new and fine, till none knows its lean old carcass."*
— Henrik Ibsen

As part of getting lost more permanently, some people establish a new identity. Sometimes they use an "assumed name." With their new name, they will have to consider obtaining fake identification, or fake ID.

Again, the publisher and author are not attorneys, are not providing legal advice, and do not recommend that anyone break any laws. This book reports what others have done.

Some people have nicknames, such as "Clint" for Clinton, "Bob" or "Rob" for Robert, "Rich" or "Dick" for Richard, "Betty" or "Liz" for Elizabeth, "Nan" or "Nance" for Nancy, etc. Part of establishing fake ID is to have a new name. People can pick a name out of thin air. Usually, people use a slight variation of their real name. Someone with a name like John A. Doe may use J.A. Doe, Jon A. Doe, John Doe, Jon Doe, J. Allen Doe, etc. Such variations in the spelling of a first or last name could be enough to "change" most identities. As a further example, Jones could be Jhones, Jons, or Johns. Smith could be Smithe, Smyth, Smit, or Smythe.

One can become another person very easily. Steps used in creating a new you may involve a new birth certificate. Some people also use a high school diploma, college degree, union membership card, Social Security card, ID card or drivers license. Depending on how thorough a person wants to be, they could have documents to cover part or all of the above. If John A. Doe's Social Security card number is 000-00-0000, he could obtain a Social Security card that shows Jon A. Doe, 000-00-0000.

It would look like a typographical error happened when they typed the name John. In the meantime, an employer would report wages to the proper Social Security account. Sometime in the future, John could point out the "error" and have it corrected. Similarly, Jon A. Doe could appear on all the other documents and identification.

There are many companies in the business of selling mail order fake ID. The quality ranges from very marginal to very high quality. There are three types of ID. The first type is "generic ID." In this case, "generic" means plain or ordinary, and without a photo. Items such as a "normal appearing" Social Security card, union membership card, library card, etc., are examples of generic ID. The second type of ID is "Photo ID." Photo ID can be of any type, accompanied by a photo. The photo is affixed to the card. Then the card is laminated. The third type of ID is "photo-positive ID." Photo-positive ID is part of the actual ID card. An example is the type of drivers license issued by most states. Some photo-positive ID comes unlaminated. However, someone can laminate the ID.

Most people agree that photo-positive ID looks more realistic. Some people provide a color photo, or possibly a black and white photo, of themselves. This photo is the type that comes from a photo machine. People find photo booths at fairs and some larger grocery stores. People pay about $2 to $4 and sit in front of a photo machine inside the booth. The machine provides about four photos. People select the best photo and send it to the fake ID company, which takes a photo of your photo. They develop that photo as part of the ID — pretty simple and the result is very realistic.

Most ID companies will have more to offer than just one type of ID. Indeed, there are "kits" or package deals you can purchase. You can obtain a birth certificate and several pieces of ID. Remember, a birth certificate or birth registration would usually show some signs of wear or age. Some people leave the document in direct sunlight, to cause some fading. Also, some people apply little drops of water in a few spots. You must be careful not to let it fade too much. Some people fold it in half, or into thirds. It looks like they had it in a Bible or safe deposit box. That adds a good touch to the "authentic look."

Most people pay attention to the age the documents should have, then match the technology of those times. As an example, a birth certificate from the late 1940s will have a certain look. There were no electric typewriters or felt pens back then. When completing the forms, people will want to be sure to use an older, manual typewriter with cloth ribbon. Usually, people signed documents with fountain pens. (Ball point pens were not around yet.) People examine other documents from the same time. They do this to check on style and appearance, so they can make their fake documents look real.

If people are into their twenties or older, they may not need an ID that shows a date of birth or their age. People must examine their purpose for a fake ID. Do most people buy a fake ID to show they are 21 years old by a few months? Do people buy a fake ID to show they are Jon A. Smith?

There are new state and federal regulations designed to crack down on businesses that make and sell fake ID. All ID which shows date of birth or age, sent or delivered by or through interstate or foreign mail, must say "not a government document" on it. However, many companies continue to sell fake ID without a birth date, without the statement, "NOT A GOVERNMENT DOCUMENT." Some of the ID, without age or date of birth, can look *very authentic*. If the fake ID does not show an age, so what? A person can say that they, too, have wondered why they didn't put their date of birth on the document.

There is a tendency for most people to be gullible about *anything in writing*. If people "see it in writing," they believe it is true, more often than not. Con men are always providing a "written guarantee" to cover their shoddy or non-existent work or product. Somehow, it reassures the victim or "mark" that everything is *legitimate*. Similarly, a photo-positive ID, with the person's name, address and an expiration date, looks very legitimate. The more identification people have that looks authentic, the more they will appear "real."

Some folks establishing new identity will start from the beginning. This involves a lot of research, and sometimes, money.

The person picks their hometown or some other city and heads for the library. The library has newspapers, whether on file in the basement, or on microfilm. There could be papers covering the time when the person seeking ID was born.

Next, the person checks the obituary information, seeking the notice of the death of a child born about the same time as the person seeking ID. (This sounds gruesome doesn't it? It is!).

Then the person must discover where that child was born. Upon learning that information, the person phones the hospital and asks about the procedure to get a duplicate birth certificate. That person explains that he is that child and that a fire destroyed his original birth certificate.

(Note: In the past several years, hospitals and government agencies have made it more difficult to get copies of birth certificates in such circumstances. Also, obtaining such a birth certificate could be against the law.)

Obtaining ID in that way is described in the book, *Reborn In The USA*. If a person is successful in obtaining a birth certificate in this manner, they will have an authentic birth certificate in the dead child's name. The person, in effect, assumes the identity that the dead child is no longer using. By obtaining other ID information, including a fake Social Security card, the person will be ready to live a new life. People could apply for a Social Security card for the first time at a late age.

It is not easy for someone to apply for a Social Security card under those circumstances. The people at Social Security will investigate your application very carefully. The person would have to answer "no" to many questions. Affirming you are telling the truth on government documents is a serious matter. If you lie, it could cause you big problems later.

If your new location has good public transportation, you may not need to have a drivers license. A "personal identification" type of ID may suffice. It is not uncommon for non-drivers to have photo-positive personal ID. If someone asks why they don't have a drivers license, the person responds that he or she can't drive. Then they mention it has something to do with blackouts, or they prefer to walk or take the bus! There is nothing wrong with any of those excuses.

Most people will agree that a person's new ID should have a birth certificate or church baptismal record. There should also be a photo-positive ID card, Social Security card, and one or more other types of ID. One of those should have a photo. Usually, someone wants to see two pieces of ID, such as a drivers license and credit card. If people do not have credit cards, they can always reply that they do have two pieces of photo-positive ID. That will usually settle any ID questions. Some people further establish their new identity by getting school documents. This includes a high school diploma or a college degree. There is more information about these items in the next chapter.

When people select and order fake ID, they make sure to have the items sent in care of a "friend" (themself). They use the street address where they live before the move. There are two reasons for this. First, the company they are dealing with will have an address that will soon be a dead end. Second, if authorities investigate that company, the old street address will be all that shows.

Most people DO NOT have this type of mail sent to their new P.O. Box "mailing address." Otherwise, they may receive a small yellow slip of paper in their box. It says they need to pick up a package. The window clerk could leave for a few minutes to "look" for their package. When the clerk returns, there could be a postal inspector or security agent with them. People do not usually want to risk such an incident.

Working within the "system," many criminals and others have a new identity with the Witness Protection Program. How many people benefit from this? Only the government knows for sure, and no one talks about it. You can bet the drivers license or ID card of former organized crime gang members does not have "NOT A GOVERNMENT DOCUMENT" stamped across the face of it.

People must obtain the best looking, most authentic ID possible. That will increase their chances of living their new identity without any problems. However, people must remember that it is the little error or slip up that can cause big problems. Fake ID is simple to get. People can do something very elaborate, or something very simple.

If you want to get fake ID, you must be very careful. You do not want to do anything that will break any laws. Only you know what needs to be done to increase your chances of success. You now realize how people get or make fake ID. If you move far enough away from your present location, you may not need to have new identification. In the Smith example, they moved a short distance and did not require new identity.

12
ESTABLISHING A FAKE JOB HISTORY

"There is properly no history, only biography."
— Emerson
"What you do not know well, relate as if you knew it well."
— Ovid

It would be good to have a job waiting for you in your new location. However, this may not be possible. You may have to move, then find a job. During your job search, you may have to develop a fake job history. There are two ways to stack the cards in your favor. Both methods involve some risk. You will have to select the method that suits your needs. Remember, many employers make only a casual reference check of past employment. Some employers will not check your past employment at all. It depends on the sort of job you want. Obviously, the lower paying jobs with high turnover might not have the background check of an engineer or scientist.

It is interesting to note that some of America's largest business firms have had their foundations rocked by the scandal of "non-qualified" employees. Some people with little scientific education have passed for engineers, scientists, and medical doctors. Other people with no management experience or education have passed for management experts. These incidents give substance to the theory that many employers simply *do not* check references. Also, it proves that many employers seldom do in-depth reference checks. Small businesses are more likely than large companies to be more thorough in checking references. You have to "key" the type of fake job history you plan to develop. Keep in mind the size of the potential employers you plan to contact. Remember the likelihood of careful screening of your application by those employers.

There are many thousands of people employed now in jobs they got with fake job histories. Most job applicants "stretch the truth" or embellish heir background a little, to make it sound better. However, there are people who lie completely about their past work experience. How did these people get their jobs? Most of them did an excellent job of selling themselves during the interview.

Through a variety of tactics, including bluffing and intimidation, the job applicant successfully played the job hunting game. Job hunting is like a card game. When you place your application before the employer (making the bet), you are either bluffing or playing with a good hand.

The first method of developing a job history is simple. Make one up out of thin air. To do this, you will need to have some knowledge about the background needed for the job you want. Ideally, you should have some previous experience with the job you seek. It is not uncommon for large companies to be very slow at checking an applicant's past work history. Out of state employment verification is typically done by mail. When it is done by phone, the person making the call may not get an immediate answer to questions about a former employee's work history. If you need to pick a firm out of thin air, you could try a large, out of state company.

When you must name your former supervisor, make up a name. Then say that the person died just before you left. You do not know who the replacement is. An alternative is to say the supervisor left to take a job with another company. That firm could be a competitor. However, you do not know the name of the firm, or where it is. Such statements might make your prospective employer reluctant to contact the firm for a reference. The person most likely to verify your abilities is no longer there. This might cause the new employer to skip that reference.

On the other hand, you could have an out of state relative or friend help you. They will pretend to be the former supervisor and verify your work history. The friend or relative would have to answer the phone as XYZ Company for quite some time. Many firms answer their phone by repeating the last four digits of their phone number, such as "5829." Your friend or relative would have to be careful until the verification call came. This could be a few days to several weeks.

If you are trying to hide, you do not want a prospective employer contacting your former employers. It is not a good idea for someone from your past to know your approximate present whereabouts. Most collections investigators will check with former employers. There could be a forwarding address for W-2 information for your tax returns. If you are ending employment with a firm and expect to leave the area, ask them to provide you with a W-2 for the year to date. They might not like the idea. However, you do have the right to receive the W-2. It just means that someone in the office will have to do a little extra work on your behalf. The employer might try to get out of doing this, so stand firm. Insist that it is your right to have the form.

The employer also may try to get your forwarding address. Tell them you do not know where you are going or for how long. You could say that you expect to do some traveling and could be in eight or ten places before the end of the year. You could say you will be traveling abroad, and will have to file your tax return from Europe. Also, you could have the W-2 mailed to a trusted friend or relative, or to the P.O. Box "mailing address." Some of these actions could lead an investigator to your area and eventually to you. It is better to pick up the W-2 in person when you leave employment, or toward the end of January. (They must mail the W-2s by the end of January.)

If you do go in person, remember to tell everyone that you are living near Yellowstone National Park. Then you say that you are going to move to Hackensack, New Jersey, next week. Two weeks later, you will be in El Centro, California. If you "travel to enough places," people will get confused. They will have no information about your real location.

If you are on the job for awhile, and complete your probationary period, most employers will not fire you because they cannot verify your past employment. On the other hand, what happens if the employment verification comes back negative? The former employer says, "we do not know this person," or, "we have no record of this employee at ABC Company." Your new employer will want to discuss the matter with you.

Depending on the circumstances, you may have to level with your supervisor and say you did not tell the truth about your last job. You could say that you had the desire, some experience, and that you made up your last job so you could get this job. This could get you fired. On the other hand, some employers may admire your courage and your abilities, and give you a break. Remember, the less you say, the better off you will be. Also, "people's plans fail, only because they fail to plan." You have to think about this very carefully.

The second method of establishing a fake job history involves some elaborate planning and some money. You can get some help from the following businesses: telephone answering services, mail drop services, secretarial services, and office buildings that offer "full service" offices. At each of these businesses, for a fee, you will have access to mail delivery and telephone answering, or both. Most of those businesses have secretarial support available.

An excellent choice is the "full service" office where you typically rent an office space. Usually, they will also rent some office furniture to you. For an additional fee, there is secretarial support, copiers and fax machines. The receptionist receives your incoming phone calls and mail. That person also will make phone calls and mail letters on your behalf.

By establishing one, two, or possibly three such "addresses" in different cities, you can make a *job history tracking*. For example: Someone in California can start with Sacramento, then San Jose, then go to San Francisco. While in Sacramento for three years, you worked at Youbetcha Company. From there you went to San Jose and worked at Hadajobthere for almost five years. Then you worked in San Francisco at WhydidIgothere Company for the last two years to the present. Wherever you go within the same state or out of state, you can list a "former employer" and dates of employment.

It is very simple to get typesetting done. A simple name and address for letterhead and envelopes may cost from $15 to $30. Some copy centers offer this service. They use computers to make the letterhead materials. The cost will probably be less than a typesetting shop. Check around and see who has a good price.

With your typeset or computer-generated "letterhead masters" in hand, you then find an inexpensive printer. You could have a copy center print some "letterheads" for you. Again, check around to see who has a favorable price. Some printers will not do small jobs, others will. A print shop will be expensive, compared to making copies. All printers will tell you about cleaning the press after each job, the set up charge, and the cost of paper. While some of this is true, most of it is horse manure. Especially if you use black ink. Remember, you will want something that looks good and is reasonable in cost. Some printers have a "business special" consisting of a certain amount of letterhead, envelopes, invoices and business cards for a set price. This could be a good bet.

Once you have your letterhead and envelopes, you will "be in business" at your secretarial service locations. When you apply for a new job, you list the "former employers," giving the name of the company and the address of the secretarial services. If there is a reference check by phone or in writing, you can find out about it by staying in contact with your offices. You will be able to respond, or have someone respond for you. They will have the appropriate information in the form of an excellent job referral. The one you made.

Of course, if you listed H.R. Simpson as your immediate supervisor at Youbetcha Company, you would want to make sure your secretary in Sacramento remembered to take a message for Mr. Simpson. "Oh, I am sorry, but Mr. Simpson is out of town on business for the next two weeks. Can anyone else help you?" If the caller asks about the personnel director, the secretary will ask, "May I ask what this is about?" The caller might say he needs an employment verification for Joe Gagootz. Then the secretary asks, did Mr. Gagootz work for Mr. Simpson? The caller responds with a yes. "Well, Mr. Simpson will have to take care of that. If I can take your name and address, I will have Mr. Simpson put the verification in writing. I will see to it that he takes care of this as soon as he gets back from his trip." How could someone doing a reference check not go along with that? Of course, success will depend on the cooperation of your secretary.

As part of a fake job history, some people need a little educational background to go with their new résumé. The book *Fraudulent Credentials* contains much information on how people acquire fake college diplomas, including reproductions of advertisements by many companies that sell diplomas by mail. Also, you may have to show your transcript. You will have to inquire about a transcript for the background you need. A photocopy of a genuine transcript does not look very good anyhow. Therefore, your copy should look acceptable to anyone requiring that type of information. Do not let them keep your copy. Insist they make their own copy. The more generations you have in making copies, the more fuzzy the details look.

If you have reasonable work experience in a particular field, and have set up your "former employers" and "college education" properly, the chances are you will not get caught. Some people do get caught. A few years ago, someone had a fake Ph.D. and a top job in a school district. He got caught and resigned the job, just ahead of getting fired. Remember, very few employers actually take the time to verify your college degree, especially if you have a "transcript" of your courses. Some employers will want to see that Social Security card. If you have already taken care of this, there should be no problem.

Now you know what some people do to establish fake ID and a fake job history. You know the necessary resources to get the job done. Now you must think about your particular situation and decide on a course of action. Remember, it is one matter to get lost for a few months in order to think about your situation. It is another matter to get lost permanently. Do not violate any laws in the process if you decide to get lost permanently.

13
Conclusion

"They fail, and they alone, who have not striven."
— Thomas Bailey Aldrich

Some Last Reminders If You Plan To Get Lost!

Do not list your name in the phone book.

Do not list your name in a city directory.

Do not give any information to a credit bureau.

Do not give any information to a collection agency.

Do not order a phone in your name — get it in the name of a friend or relative.

Do not receive mail at your street address.

Do not give information to relatives or friends.

Do not have your street address on your drivers license.

Do not give your new address to the schools.

Do not use your real name for newspaper subscriptions.

Do not use credit cards or charge cards.

Do not sign for open use of your medical records.

Do not travel by bus or airline.

Do not tell your neighbors where you are moving.

Do not give a street address on pet licenses.

Do not drive a particularly noticeable car.

Do not initiate mail-forwarding to your new street address.
Do not use a big-name mover.
Do not become too friendly with your new landlord or neighbors.
Do not skip town owing rent or utilities.
Do not throw or attend loud parties.
Do not register to vote.
Any of these actions can lead an investigator to you.

Missing Persons

Throughout the years, many people have disappeared, either by their own choosing or foul play. Some of the disappearances are very unusual. In the book, *Thin Air, The Life And Mysterious Disappearance Of Helen Brach,* Pat Colander mentions some very strange "beam me up" situations.

One incident involved the leader of a gang of bandits. After pillaging a town, the mob of 100 bandits rode off, following their leader. The leader was some distance ahead of the pack. One moment, their leader was riding ahead of them. The next moment, his horse was riderless. They never found the leader.

Another episode involved a prisoner who was walking with a group of fellow inmates. They had shackles and chains, and walked in single file. The man seemed to fade, slowly, in front of everyone, and then became invisible. He literally disappeared into thin air.

In another situation, a man was running in front of two friends. He stumbled and fell. Before he touched the ground, he vanished into thin air.

Another case involved a man who went to get some water at the spring. His foot tracks were in the freshly fallen snow. He did not return from a task that would normally take just a few minutes. His family searched for him. They followed his foot tracks in the snow and saw where the tracks abruptly ended, with no further trace of the man.

In his book, *Among The Missing,* Jay Robert Nash details many people who have disappeared over the years. In the cases of the more famous persons who "get lost" or disappear, there is a likelihood of foul play. These persons include: Dorothy Arnold, niece of U.S.

Supreme Court Justice Rufus Peckham; Baroness F.C. Von Cottendorf; Judge Joseph Force Crater; Amelia Earhart; Michael Clark Rockefeller; James Riddle Hoffa; and Helen Vorhees Brach.

A recent development occurred with the Helen Vorhees Brach matter. After 18 years, police arrested a man in connection with the case. Police claim there was a horse-trading scam. Apparently, Helen Brach found out about the scam and threatened to inform the police. Shortly thereafter, she disappeared. The man is in custody. Others are coming forward, saying he scammed them too.

Since the 1960s, there have been many people who have decided to "get lost." Many years later, people sometimes "discover" the missing person. Others come out of hiding on their own. During subsequent interviews, these people mentioned their desire to get lost and start a new life. The main theme was a focus on a fresh start in a new location, usually with a new identity. These people, tired of their previous existence, wanted another chance at life. Again, good luck with your particular choice of action. Remember, avoid breaking any laws.

Hard Times

Remember, during and following a period of recession, three events happen: One is *business failure*, another is *worker displacement,* and the last is *an increase in consumer spending.* Also, there tends to be an increase in suicide attempts.

During a recession, large corporations often take steps to modernize their plants, equipment and facilities. The new equipment and methods often lead to worker displacement. That means workers lose their jobs. As the future unfolds, robotics will take the place of many workers. Displacement happens as a result of the increased modernization of productivity. There are very few segments of the work force that will be immune to displacement. The displacement will range from office workers to factory workers.

```
┌─────────────────────────┐
│  U. S. BUSINESS         │
│  FAILURES               │
│  1982 —24,908           │
│  1983—31,334            │
│  1984—52,078            │
│  1985—57,253            │
│  1986—61,616            │
│  1987—61,111            │
│  1988—57,908            │
│  1989—50,361            │
│  1990—66,747            │
│  1991—88,140            │
│  1992—96,857            │
│  Source: 113th Edition  │
│  Statistical Abstract of│
│  The United States, 1993│
│  As reported by         │
│  Dun and Bradstreet Corp.│
└─────────────────────────┘
```

Figure 6

Once people who have been unemployed go back to work, there is an increase in spending. These people want to purchase many items they have gone without for months or years. This is partly due to their increased income. Cars, appliances, many household items, and personal luxury items find their way home. The quick result is an increase in debt.

Again, based on certain income levels, the newly-rehired consumers get credit. Again, they are encouraged to spend money they really do not have. The total effect of displacement, and getting back to work for some, is continually increasing consumer debt. Also, there are bouts of unemployment. Therefore, while the economic recovery might be a sign of a return to the good times, for many it is not. That is why the information in the book is so important.

One sign of slow times is a reduction in domestic automobile production. Since 1985, there has been a gradual reduction in U.S. passenger car production. Is this an economic forecasting model?

During this time, the government kept telling us how good the economy was doing. Looks like the auto manufacturers did not believe the political hot talk.

U.S. PASSENGER CAR PRODUCTION

1980	6,376,000
1985	8,185,000
1986	7,829,000
1987	7,100,000
1988	7,137,000
1989	6,825,000
1990	6,078,000
1991	5,440,000

**Source: 113th Edition
Statistical Abstract of
The United States, 1993**

Figure 7

In November of 1985, the seed germinated. By mid-1988, the bush (no pun intended) started to grow. By that I mean there was grave concern about the economy for the coming ten years. There was some economic recovery in the past few years. However, large corporations have cut their work forces by millions of employees. In May of 1988, consumer debt reached an all time high. Since that time, it continues to grow to new all time highs, through mid-1995.

The result of all this may be another SEVERE recession, or a depression. The cycle appears to perpetuate itself. The main problem is the inability of Congress to deal with the domestic deficit and the foreign trade imbalance. When the government runs out of money, they print more money. That makes everyone's money worth less.

When you run out of money, that's it! You can't print more money, without great risk of long confinement. The past is the past. It is something to learn from and to use as a building block.

Remember, the publisher and author are not attorneys. We do not provide any legal advice. We do not advocate the breaking of any laws. Certain activities described in this book could be against local, state or federal laws. It is best to check with an attorney before you choose a course of action. This book reports information about what others have done to get lost or ditch their debts. We do not recommend that you follow the same actions.

DEATHS BY SUICIDE		
	MALE	**FEMALE**
1970	16,629	6,851
1980	20,505	6,364
1985	23,145	6,308
1987	24,272	6,524
1988	24,078	6,329
1989	24,102	6,130
1990	24,724	6,182

Source: 113th Edition, Statistical Abstract
of The United States, 1993

Figure 8

Remember, no amount of debt is worth ending your life. Too many people kill themselves during bad financial times. Many of these people could not cope with the stress and depression of unemployment, or the lack of adequate income to meet their expenses. Many of these people could not handle the constant harassment by the collection system.

Some people may criticize others who are not able to manage their finances or who have debts in collection. Some people take a dim view of bankruptcy. These folks probably have no idea what it is like to experience long term inability to deal with debt. If you have good, steady income, you do not have to worry about debts. If their income stopped, they would have a very different attitude about the matter.

Regardless of how bad the situation gets, it is not worth killing yourself. Bankruptcy can rescue you and give you another chance.

If you choose to get lost or ditch your debts, I hope you can recover, go forward, and prosper. My best wishes are with you, and I hope your future is Healthy, Happy and Prosperous.

Appendix
Recommended Reading

How To Find A Job

The last thirty years saw hundreds of books published about how to find a job and related subject areas. While the following list is not all-inclusive, it is a reasonable list of reading material to help you make choices. The list shows the title, author, publisher and year published.

Nearly all of these books are at your local library. If the library does not have a book, they could get it from another library. Some of these books may go "out of print." That means your average book store will not be able to order the book. However, certain book stores specialize in out-of-print books. Also, you can try used book stores.

Most libraries have a rotation system, which keeps books for a specified time. Then the library discontinues the book. Sometimes, a library may keep a book practically forever. If your local library cannot find a book for you, ask them if they can order it. Your library may be able to borrow the book from another library in or out of the state where you live.

Here are some books and videotapes you may find useful.

Résumés that Get Jobs, Joan Reed, Prentice Hall, 1991.

The Best Jobs for the 1990s and Into the 21st Century, Ronald L. Krannish, Caryl Rae Krannish, Impact Publications, 1993.

America's Top Technical and Trade Jobs, J. Michael Farr, JIST, 1991.

An Easier Way to Change Jobs, Bob Serberg, Princeton/Masters Press, 1993.

Résumés Don't Get Jobs, Bob Weinstein, McGraw-Hill, 1993.

Jobs '93, Kathryn Petras, Simon & Schuster, 1993.

What Smart People Do When Losing Their Jobs, Kathleen A. Richle, Wiley, 1991.

How to Locate Jobs And Land Interviews, Albert L. French, Career Press, 1993.

Winning the Job You Really Want, Taylor Taylor, Almon Productions, 1992.

America's Fastest Growing Employers: The Complete Guide to Finding Jobs with Over 700 of America's Hottest Companies, Carter Smith, Bob Adams, Inc., 1992.

Where The Jobs Are: The Hottest Careers for the '90s, Mark Satterfield, Career Press, 1992.

How to Locate Jobs and Land Interviews: A Complete Guide, Reference, and Resource Book — for the "Job Hunter" — , Albert L. French, High Pine Publishers, 1991.

Guide to Cruise Ship Jobs, George Reilly, Pilot Books, 1991.

Credit And Credit Problem Solving

There are many books about credit and credit problem solving. The following list is a reasonable selection of reading material. I do not know all the answers, and I am suspicious of people who say they know all the answers. The more you read about solving credit problems, the better informed you will be. Again, your local library should have these books in stock or be able to order them for you.

You and Your Credit: Tools for Understanding & Repairing Your Own Credit, Darryl R. White, Pyramid Publishers, 1994.

The Guerrilla Guide to Credit Repair: How to Find Out What's Wrong with Your Credit Rating — and How to Fix It, Todd Bierman, St. Martins', Press, 1994.

Life After Debt: How to Repair Your Credit and Get Out of Debt Once and For All, Bob Hammond, Career Press, 1993.

The Credit Repair Kit, John Ventura, Dearborn Financial Publishers, 1993.

When Money Is The Drug: The Compulsion for Credit, Cash and Chronic Debt, Donna Bundy, Harper San Francisco, 1993.

The Ultimate Credit Handbook, Gerri Detweiler, Penguin Books, 1993.

How to Get a Line of Credit for Your Business, Bryan E. Milling, Sourcebooks, 1993.

Downsize Your Debt: How to Take Control of Your Personal Finances, Andrew Feinberg, Penguin, 1993.

Fresh Start: Surviving Money Troubles, Rebuilding Your Credit, Recovering Before or After Bankruptcy, John Ventura, Dearborn Financial Publications, 1992.

Privacy for Sale: How Computerization Has Made Everyone's Private Life an Open Secret, Jeffrey Rothfeder, Simon & Schuster, 1992.

Debtor's Rights: A Legal Self-Help Guide with Forms, Sudrun M. Nickel, Sphinx International, 1992.

When Spending Takes The Place of Feeling, Karen O'Connor, T. Nelson, 1992.

Money Troubles: Legal Strategies to Cope with Your Debts, Robin Leonard, Nolo Press, 1991.

The Meyers Guide to Consumer Bankruptcy, J. I. Meyers, Legal Express, 1991.

Credit Mechanic:The Poor Man's Guide to Credit Repair, J. Arlene White, Paladin Press, 1991.

Kiplinger's Guide to Family Finances, Conrad Productions, 1991.

How to Erase Bad Credit: A Nanual for the Credit Impaired, Stanley R. Stern & David Waldman, Law Kits, 1990.

The Check Is Not in The Mail, Leonard Sklar, Baroque Publishers, 1990.

Bankruptcy

There are many books about bankruptcy. Most of the books offer a step by step format. Also, most books include the forms necessary for someone to file bankruptcy. Most of these books are very interesting and could help you. Again, your library will be able to get any of these books for you. After you look at several, you can order one from your favorite bookstore. If you buy the book you like the best, it will serve as a reference for as long as you need it.

How to File Bankruptcy, Stephen Elias, Nolo Press, 1993.

Life After Bankruptcy: The Complete Do-It-Yourself Guide to Surviving and Prospering after Personal Bankruptcy, Charles Price, Practical Publications, 1993.

Surviving Bankruptcy: A Personal and Small Business Guide, D. S. Anderson, Prentice Hall, 1992.

How to File Your Own Bankruptcy, (or How to Avoid It), Edward A. Haman, Sphinx Publishers, 1992.

You Can Go Bankrupt Without Going Broke, An Essential Guide to Personal Bankruptcy, Lawrence, R. Reich, Pharos Books, 1992.

How to Declare Your Personal Bankruptcy Without a Lawyer, Benji O. Anosike, Do-It-Yourself Legal Publishers, 1992.

Saving Your Business: How to Survive Chapter 11 Bankruptcy and Successfully Reorganize Your Company, Suzanne Caplan, Prentice Hall, 1992.

Bankruptcy, Jack Beider and Gene Grossman, Magic Lamp Productions, 1991.

General Self-Help Information

The following books may be of interest to you.

How You Can Buy a Business Without Overpaying: More Money Left on Your Side of the Table, Gary L. Schine, Consultant Press, 1991.

Buying and Selling a Small Business, Michael M. Coltman, Self-Counsel Press, 1991.

How to Buy Almost Any Drug Legally, Without a Prescription, James H. Johnson, Avon Books, 1990.

From Bumper to Bumper, Bob Sikorsky's Best Automotive Tips, Robert Sikorsky, TAB Books, 1991.

Take It Back! The Art of Returning Almost Anything, Arlene Singer and Karen Parmet, National Press Books, 1991.

Effective Buying, Yan Moore, Beacon Films/Magic Lantern Productions, 1992.

Secrets from the Underground Shopper: The Only Book to Tell You What the Retailers Won't, Sue Goldstein, Taylor Publishing Company, 1993.

Smart Shopping and Consumerism, Rubin Saunders, Watts, 1973.

The Smart Shopper's Guide to Food Buying and Preparation, Joan Bingham and Dolores Riccio, Scribners, 1992.

Your Rights As a Consumer: Legal Tips for Savvy Purchasing of Goods, Services and Credit, Marc R. Lieberman, Career Press, 1994.

The Complete Guide to Buying a Business, Richard W. Snowden, American Management Association, 1994.

How to Buy and Manage a Franchise, Joseph Mancuso, Simon & Schuster, 1993.

Buying a Business: A Step-By-Step for the First-Time Buyer, Ronald J. McGregor, Crisp Publications, 1993.

How to Leave Your Job and Buy a Business of Your Own, Shapiro & Tomlinson, Self-Reliance Press, Inc., 1992.

Do-It-Yourself Bargain Book, How to Save 50% — and More — Buying Products and Materials, Tom Philbin, Warner Books, 1992.

The Official Government Auction Guide, George C. Chelekis, Crown, 1992.

Beat the Supermarket Blues — and Eat Well Too!, Martha Giles and Joyce Conway, Purpose Books, 1994.

How to Pinch a Penny 'Till It Screams: Stretching Your Dollars in the 90's, Rochelle L. McDonald, Avery Publishing Group, 1994.

The Super Coupon Shopping System: Ingenious New Ways to Save $$$ on Every Shopping Bill, Susan Samtur, Hyperion, 1994.

Don't Get Taken! How to Avoid Everyday Consumer Rip-Offs, Steven
  Mitchell, Consumer Reports Books, 1993.
*Financial Boot Camp: How to Avoid America's Fifteen Consumer
  Land Mines,* James L. Paris, Creation House, 1992.

Index

YOU WILL ALSO WANT TO READ: